1901 West Madison Street
Chicago, IL 60612

John McDonough, President
Jay Blunk, Executive Vice President
Adam Kempenaar, Director of New Media and Publications
John Sandberg, Coordinator, Publications
Brad Boron, New Media and Publications Assistant
Kelsey Peters, New Media and Publications Assistant
Bob Verdi, Blackhawks Historian
Chase Agnello-Dean, Coordinator, Photography

Adam Kempenaar

John Sandberg

Kelsey Peters
Brad Boron

Bob Verdi

Anne E. Stein

Chris Weibring

Chase Agnello-Dean
Bill Smith
Rudi Ayasse
Kena Krutsinger
Getty Images

Rock Communications
1117 East 14th St. North
Newton, IA 50208

Color FX
10776 Aurora Ave.
Des Moines, IA 50322
www.colorfxprint.com

Triumph Books
542 S. Dearborn St., Suite 750
Chicago, IL 60605

TRIUMPH
B O O K S

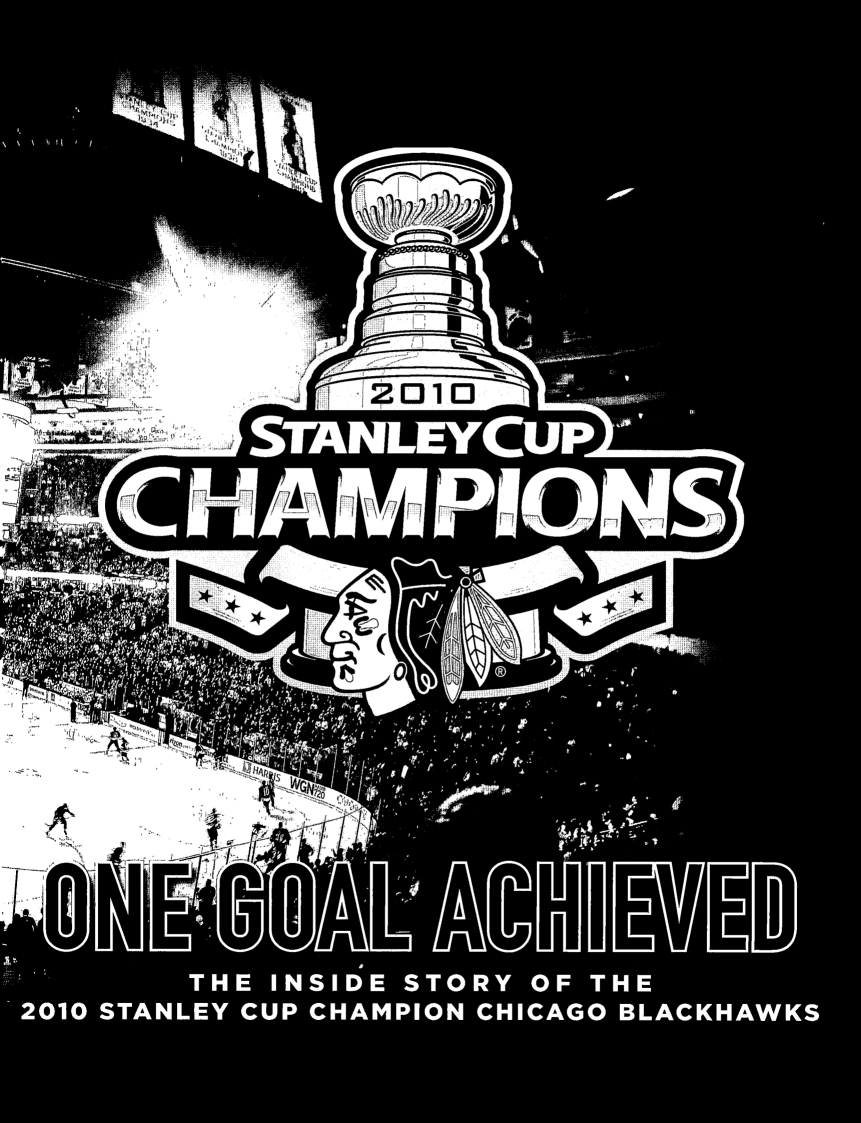

2010
STANLEY CUP
CHAMPIONS

ONE GOAL ACHIEVED

THE INSIDE STORY OF THE
2010 STANLEY CUP CHAMPION CHICAGO BLACKHAWKS

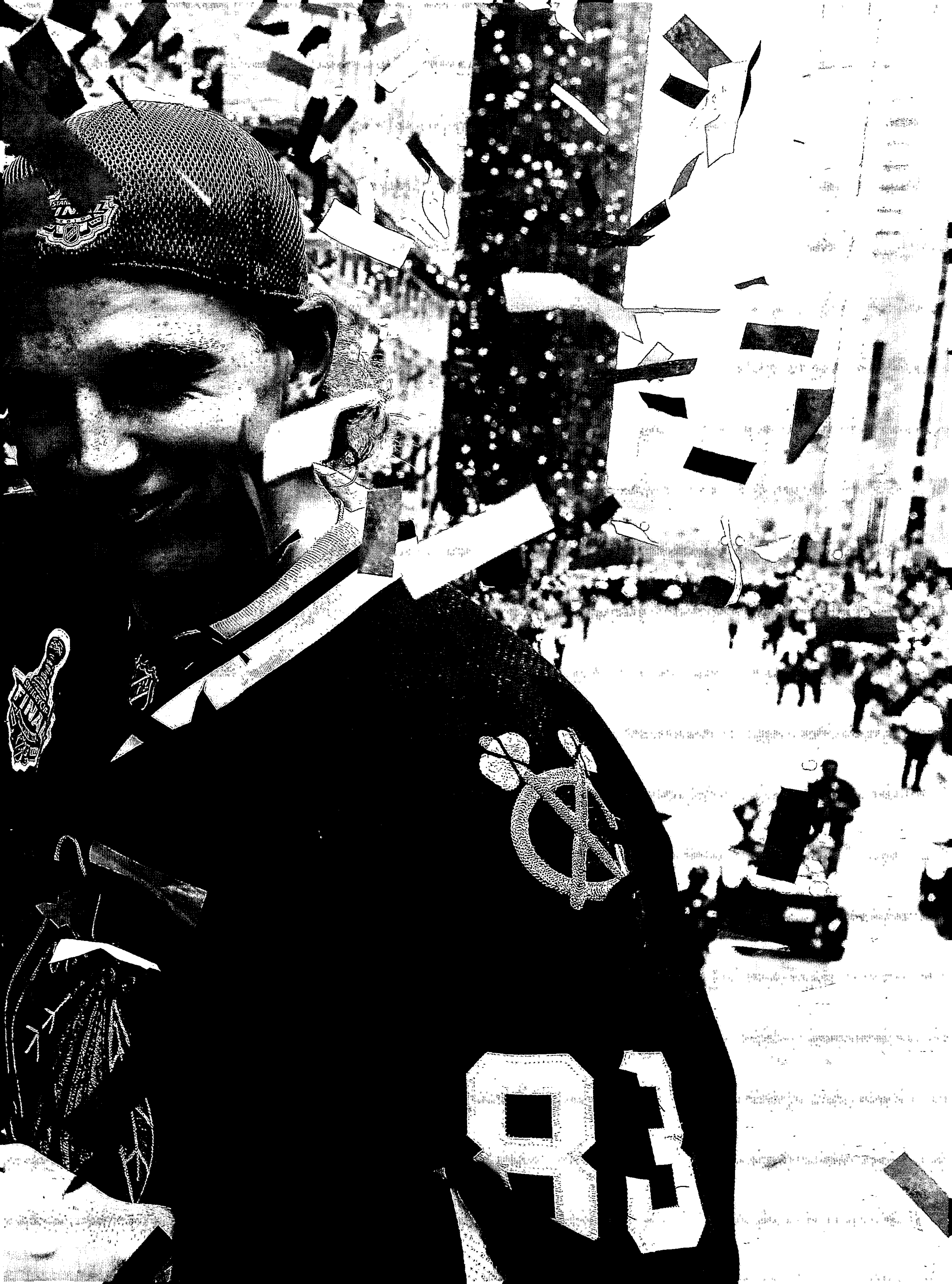

FRONT ROW:
Cristobal Huet, Brad Aldrich,
Dave Knickerbocker, Dale Tallon,
John Torchetti, Kevin Cheveldayoff,
Scotty Bowman, Joel Quenneville,
Stan Bowman, Rocky Wirtz,
Jonathan Toews, John McDonough,
Jay Blunk, Al MacIsaac, Mike Haviland,
Chris Werner, Adam Kempenaar,
Paul Vincent, TJ Skattum,
Steve Waight, Stephane Waite, Antti Niemi

SECOND ROW:
Brandon Faber, Kim Johnsson,
Trisha Ithal, Jim Bare, Duncan Keith,
Bob Verdi, Kayla Kindred,
Adam Rogowin, Elizabeth Queen,
Annie Camins, Patricia Walsh,
Jillian Smith, Tony Ommen,
Mark McGuire, Patrick Kane,
Rich Sommers, Ian Gentile,
Morgan Sharar-Stoppel, Dan Rozenblat,
Paul Goodman, Emily Jungles,
Marie Sutera, Clint Reif

THIRD ROW:
Julie Lovins, Liz Breuer,
Kelly Smith, Troy Brouwer,
Anne Brannen, Steve DiLenardi,
Patrick Sharp, Jake Tuton,
Eric Dumais, Paul Kennedy,
AJ Dolan, Tracy Cunningham,
Leanne Mayville, Marian Hossa,
Tom Phelan, Ashley Hinton,
Janelle Miller, Aaron Salsbury,
Andrew Ladd, Alex Seaton,
John Madden, Sean Keefer,
Pawel Prylinski, Kevin Haas

GO BLACKHAWKS

FOURTH ROW:
Jim Heintzelman, Troy Parchman,
Brent Sopel, Jeff Thomas,
Corey Krawiec, Patrick Thornquist,
Greg Zinsmeister, Patrick Dahl,
Allison Westfall, Troy Murray,
Brian Campbell, Pat Foley,
Kris Versteeg, Judd Sirott,
John Sandberg, Dave Bolland,
Scott Hanson, Andy Roan,
Adam Burish, TR Johnson,
Kyleen King, Joe Doyle,
Brent Seabrook, Matthew Dominick

TOP ROW:
Chase Agnello-Dean, Dustin Byfuglien,
Chris Weibring, Sara Bailey,
Michael Dorsch, Colin Fraser,
Eddie Olczyk, Brad Chase,
Niklas Hjalmarsson, Dave Olson,
Brian Dahm, Steve McNelley,
Brian Howe, Mike Gapski,
Brad Boron, James Gary,
Nick Zombolas, Jordan Hendry,
John Wiedeman, Lauren Lang,
Tomas Kopecky, Julie Kavanaugh,
Ben Eager, Pete Hassen

NOT PICTURED:
Dr. Michael Terry, Tom O'Grady,
Shilpa Rupani, Ryan Linich,
Zack Bero, Katie Stankiewicz

TABLE OF CONTENTS

INTRODUCTION

CHAPTER 1

THE ART OF WORK 19

CHAPTER 2

THINKING BIG 43

CHAPTER 3

THE QUEST BEGINS 69

FOREWORD

When I received a phone call from Rocky Wirtz in November of 2007, I thought it was just a get-acquainted call. When we sat down a few days later for what turned into a five-hour lunch, I found out it was much more than that.

About an hour in he said something that changed my life: "I'm going to lose all my leverage when I say this, but I want you to run the Blackhawks." Not only did he not lose any leverage, he gained all of my respect.

The past three years have been an amazing journey that has been defined by profound cultural change. We're trying to build an elite organization that represents a "Blackhawks Way" of doing things. This includes winning, strong communication, big picture thinking and a collaboration of business and hockey operations.

At the center of all of this change is the team we have on the ice. It is very exhilarating to see the young nucleus come together, mature and develop into a champion. Chicago has now become a destination for free agents who believe their career will be enhanced if they play for the Blackhawks.

It is also very important that I acknowledge the remarkable support we have received from our fans. The United Center experience is something that is simply awe-inspiring and fuels the coaches and players every night. We are grateful that you gave us another chance, and we will do everything we can to reward your allegiance. We want to ensure that, in fact, the pride is back, and we will not take anything for granted.

I am very proud of the progress this organization has made. The Stanley Cup championship has provided our fans with unforgettable memories and a summer of seismic celebration. But I realize that there is always more to accomplish.

We will continue on our path of sustained excellence and work toward our "One Goal."

— John F. McDonough is president of the Chicago Blackhawks

BY W. ROCKWELL WIRTZ

More than 20,000 fans filled the Wachovia Center for Game 6 of the 2010 Stanley Cup Final, and more than 5 million watched the game on television in the U.S. Though I was in the stadium that night, you may be surprised to know that I fell mostly into the latter category, especially as the game wore on. Too nervous to watch the 3-3 game going late into regulation, I paced around our box, looking over to the monitor every time I heard the crowd react.

Expectations are funny. We entered the 2009-10 season knowing that, should everything go right, we had a real chance at the Cup. But at that moment, with the season on the line and a tied game, I did everything I could to lower my expectations; better to let the excitement wash over me if we won rather than to be disappointed if we needed a seventh game.

Win or lose, we had come so far in such a short amount of time. Many in Chicago would have never even thought this was possible just a few years ago.

It was more than just a few years ago that I fell in love with hockey, which is easy to do when some of your earliest memories include Bobby, Stan, "Tony O" and the old Chicago Stadium. Every Sunday home game (weekdays were school nights, of course), I came downtown to watch the city's most exciting team as fans cheered so loud the building shook. The Blackhawks took Chicago by storm.

When it came time to take over the team in 2007, I knew that the best way to honor my father, uncle, grandfather and every other Blackhawks fan, all of whom loved the team as much as I did, was to bring the electricity and excitement that I felt as a boy back to Chicago. John McDonough and I made expectations our mantra: We charged our team and front office with lofty goals and high expectations, and in return we'd give them the best resources to meet them — the best facilities, the best scouts, the best accommodations, the best everything.

The moment I knew we were on the right track happened more than two years before Jonathan Toews hoisted the Cup. With the season winding down and just a few too many points out of the playoffs, we knew that our next game against Nashville would be the home finale to our 2007-08 season. I expected a smaller crowd; instead, we sold out every seat, and it was one of the year's loudest games. As I took my seat and looked at the 21,000 fans around me, I thought to myself, "We are on our way."

Which brings me back to Game 6. As luck would have it, Patrick Kane scored his now-famous overtime goal, the Blackhawks won the last game of the 2009-10 season and with it Lord Stanley's Cup. Standing at center ice, holding the Cup above my head, I understood the enormity of what had happened that night: The team had defied all expectations and accomplished something great together.

This isn't an end to the story, however, just another episode in the storied history of the Chicago Blackhawks. I consider this book a down payment to the legions of passionate Blackhawks fans everywhere. Between its covers you'll find wonderful stories about this legendary franchise, but the future remains to be written. The 2010 championship was not an end — there was, and still is, more than "One Goal." Hopefully, we will continue to raise your expectations for what a professional sports team can do.

One goal has been achieved, but there are so many more to go.

— W. Rockwell Wirtz is chairman of the Chicago Blackhawks

CHAPTER ONE
THE ART OF WORK

CHICAGO BLACKHAWKS
WORLD CHAMPIONS

TIMES LATE NEWS PHOTOS
WORLD HOCKEY CHAMPS

(TIMES Photo)

Here are the four heroes who brought world title to Chicago Blackhawks after the most sensational "comeback" battle in hockey history. Scorers in the final 4-1 rout of the Toronto Maple Leafs, they portray high glee in dressing room after game. (L. to r.) Jack Shill, Carl Voss, Cully Dahlstrom and Mush March. Barely escaping cellar position as league season closed, the Miracle Hawks nosed into Stanley cup series, amazingly beat Montreal Maroons and New York Americans, then in the craziest final ever staged, defeated favorite Toronto squad 3 out of 4 games for title.

SEE NEWS OF THE WORLD IN PICTURES EVERY DAY IN
THE TIMES
CHICAGO'S PICTURE NEWSPAPER

DAILY 2c NOT 3c   SUNDAY 5c NOT 10c

Just Happened to College Football P. 16
BY AUSTIN MURPHY

MVP
Conn Smythe winner
Jonathan Toews

AT LAST!
BLACKHAWKS

CHICAGO WINS ITS
FIRST STANLEY CUP
IN 49 YEARS
BY MICHAEL FARBER P. 54

PLUS
Strasburg
Dominates P. 38
U.S. World Cup
Dreams P. 46
Mickelson's
Best Shot P. 66

MAJOR FREDERICK McLAUGHLIN in the dressing room with CHARLIE GARDINER (left) who had just registered a 1-0 shutout over the Toronto Maple Leafs to win Chicago's first Stanley Cup. Seated at right is HAROLD "MUSH" MARCH who scored the winning goal after 30' 5" of overtime.
Game played at Chicago Stadium on April 10, 1934.   COURTESY CHICAGO SUN TIMES

Chicago "Black Hawks"

THE ART OF WORK
BY BOB VERDI

Certain similarities exist when comparing the four Stanley Cups won by the Chicago Blackhawks. But to imply that there is a straight line connecting all championships would be a stretch indeed. Different eras are involved, not to mention the inevitable peaks and valleys attendant to all professional sports franchises. Quantum leaps forward automatically convey the obvious: At some point, your team was down and out.

The 1934 Blackhawks won their Cup the old-fashioned way: Harold "Mush" March, all 140 pounds of him, scored the only goal of the clinching game in the second overtime. Four years later the trip was more unconventional. The Blackhawks won only 14 of 48 regular season assignments, yet vindicated owner Major Frederick J. McLaughlin's faith in American-born players — an unfathomable strategy at the time — by winning another Cup, but not before leaning on a virtually anonymous goalkeeper.

Antti Niemi may not have been the No. 1 masked man when the Blackhawks embarked on their storied campaign in October of 2009, but Alfie Moore was not even in the building when they opened the 1938 final in Toronto, where Mike Karakas' broken toe precluded his devotion to duty. There were no "backup" goalies then, so the Blackhawks issued an all-points alert for Moore. All points led to a local watering hole, where he "joined" the squad two hours before Game 1, which he won, 3-1 — a crucial triumph that propelled the Blackhawks to a stirring conquest in the best-of-five series.

After a not-so-brief interlude, the Blackhawks seized their third Cup in 1961 — a highly therapeutic title for the franchise and its fans following a grim decade or so during which the team's record and Chicago Stadium attendance deteriorated to such a point that the NHL pondered abandoning the Windy City, perhaps for St. Louis.

"Chicago was Siberia," recalled Glenn Hall. "If you were on any of the other five teams in the league and you acted up, you were always threatened with being traded to Chicago." Hall acted up a bit in Detroit, where sidekick Ted Lindsay was trying to organize a union, and both were sent to the Blackhawks in 1957.

Finances were not a problem because the ownership of James Norris and Arthur Wirtz were wealthy and willing. But dollar bills can't skate, and the Blackhawks desperately needed bodies. General Manager Tommy Ivan, hired away from the regal Red Wings, wheeled and dealed and spent to acquire players, even if it meant buying entire minor league clubs and sponsoring amateur organizations. "If I lose $1 million a year," Norris intoned, "I can only operate the Blackhawks for two or three centuries."

Eventually the pipeline gushed with talented youngsters, notably Bobby Hull and Stan Mikita, who enriched a roster of some venerable individuals, none more important than Hall.

With "Mr. Goalie" a fixture between the pipes — working on a streak of 503 consecutive starts, a record that seems safe for only two or three centuries — the Blackhawks authored a first round upset of the Montreal Canadiens, who were seeking their sixth straight Stanley Cup, then spilled the Red Wings in a six-game final with Ab McDonald registering the game-winning goal in a 5-1 clincher.

To this day, Hull and Mikita admit they thought those Blackhawks would evolve into a dynasty, but the Stanley Cup is an elusive milestone that has become progressively more difficult to attain, what with four playoff series now required instead of two. With Hull and Mikita still carrying the baton, along with another future Hall of Fame goalie in Tony Esposito, the Blackhawks were on the cusp of a fourth Stanley Cup in 1971. They won the first two games of a theatrical final against the Montreal Canadiens, then mounted a 2-0 lead in Game 7 at the Stadium, only to succumb, 3-2, on Henri Richard's tie-breaking goal. Hull and Mikita rue that steamy evening on West Madison Street as if it happened a week ago.

"I'll never forget it," said Hull. "We let one get away, and we can't have it back."

Hull departed in 1972 for the Winnipeg Jets of the rival World Hockey Association, but with copious amounts of adrenaline, the Blackhawks surprised by advancing to the 1973 Cup final anyway. They lost to Montreal, 4 games to 2, and did not qualify for the big dance again until 1992, when they entered the final on an 11-game winning streak under coach Mike Keenan. The Blackhawks opened well against the Pittsburgh Penguins, but it was a fleeting gesture, for Mario Lemieux and company salvaged Game 1, 5-4, then completed a sweep.

During a considerable portion of the 1980s, the Blackhawks of Denis Savard and Doug Wilson understandably felt they had at least the second best team in hockey. Alas, that was the reign of Wayne Gretzky and Edmonton's mighty Oilers.

[ABOVE] Bobby Hull (left) and Jack Evans moments after the Blackhawks won the 1961 Stanley Cup.
[OPPOSITE] Stan Mikita and the Blackhawks suffered disappointing finishes in both the 1971 and 1973 Stanley Cup finals.

BOBBY HULL AND STAN MIKITA RUE THAT EVENING IN 1971 AS IF IT HAPPENED A WEEK AGO. "WE LET ONE GET AWAY, AND WE CAN'T HAVE IT BACK," SAID HULL.

IN THE LATE 1950s THE BLACKHAWKS FOUND HULL AND MIKITA. NOW THE BLACKHAWKS HAD TOEWS AND KANE.

When the Blackhawks came up against Lemieux, it felt like déjà vu.

The Blackhawks dabbled in subsequent postseasons, but appearances became fewer and futile against an assortment of stronger foes. After losing the conference quarterfinals in 1997 to Colorado, the Blackhawks faded demonstrably. Administrative alterations and serial coaching changes did not camouflage the fact that gifted players were disappearing through attrition or other means. Meanwhile quality reinforcements simply did not arrive, either in quantity or quality. When the Stadium ceded to the United Center in 1995, the new facility, about three times the size of the old one, seemed half-empty on some cold winter nights for the quaintest of reasons — it *was* half-empty, or worse.

Whether this bleak epoch could be compared with the dismal 1950s depends on one's view. With the Original Six, only five familiar adversaries existed. But as the NHL expanded to its present size of 30 franchises, identities were blurred and attachments fractured. Free agency allowed teams to bolster fortunes, but there were no guarantees that players who were bought would justify their salaries or represent actual building blocks instead of temporary relief.

As the Blackhawks languished without a discernable direction, a spate of teams won Stanley Cups — standbys such as Detroit, but also late arrivals such as Dallas and New Jersey and Tampa Bay and Carolina and Anaheim and Colorado and Pittsburgh. When the NHL shut down for the entire 2004-05 season, a drastic maneuver, the impetus and the objective was to achieve cost certainty. A hard salary cap became the way to do business, the only way to do business, a truism not lost on Dale Tallon when he was installed as general manager in June of 2005.

Unlike other sports with more flexible payroll rules, mistakes were critical because they could not easily be dismissed. Dollars were precious and, more significantly, measured down to the penny. Building from within became paramount and obsessive homework a necessity. If, for instance, the Blackhawks missed on high draft choices, and they had on, lo, too many occasions in the past, it would not matter whether home games were blacked out on television as a courtesy to season ticketholders because that breed was vanishing.

During the 2006 Entry Draft in Vancouver, the Blackhawks picked third behind St. Louis (Erik Johnson) and Pittsburgh (Jordan Staal). Tallon selected Jonathan Toews, a versatile forward who had enjoyed success playing for his native Canada in international competition and at the University of North Dakota. Blackhawks fans had been promised potential before, only to be disappointed. Toews did not disappoint. He would become the third youngest captain in NHL history and a vital component of the team's rejuvenation, as witnessed by his already crowded trophy case.

A year later the Blackhawks got lucky. Eventual Stanley Cup foe Philadelphia, having compiled their worst record ever and worst in the NHL, were in the pole position to win the draft lottery. The Blackhawks finished with the fifth fewest points and thus the least chance of jumping ahead, yet snagged the call for No. 1 and promptly grabbed Patrick Kane, a smallish

forward with an abundance of skill, courage and upside. In the late 1950s the Blackhawks found Hull and Mikita. Now they had Toews and Kane.

The Blackhawks were on their way, even if whiplashed fans were reluctant to equate that half-empty United Center with a half-full forecast.

[ABOVE] Former General Manager Dale Tallon and the Blackhawks selected Patrick Kane first overall at the 2007 NHL Entry Draft.
[OPPOSITE] Kane and Jonathan Toews have become cornerstones of the Blackhawks franchise.

[ABOVE] One of the first tasks for John McDonough (center) as Blackhawks president was to bring former players back into the fold, including Bobby Hull (left) and Stan Mikita who were named team ambassadors in a ceremony on March 7, 2008.
[OPPOSITE TOP] From left to right: Executive Vice President Jay Blunk, Mayor Richard M. Daley, McDonough and Chairman Rocky Wirtz at the Winter Classic 2009 media day.
[OPPOSITE BOTTOM] The Blackhawks and Red Wings met in the first-ever hockey game played at Wrigley Field on Jan. 1, 2009.

LUCK IS THE RESIDUE OF DESIGN. THAT IS, A WORK OF ART TENDS TO STEM FROM THE ART OF WORK.

Unrequited love for a sport and a franchise can hurt after all. But Tallon and his staff continued to fortify the roster. Patrick Sharp had already come over from Philadelphia in a 2005 midseason steal. Niklas Hjalmarsson was 108th in his draft class. Sounds low except in previous summers Dustin Byfuglien was 245th and Troy Brouwer 214th. Upstairs a culture shock was occurring. Rocky Wirtz took over as chairman in October of 2007. He hired John McDonough as president, who brought with him another business genius from the Cubs, Jay Blunk.

The product improved. The Blackhawks had a winning season but just missed the 2008 playoffs. Not good enough for the modern regime. When Niemi signed as a free agent, there was little fuss. Same as when Andrew Ladd showed up from Carolina for Tuomo Ruutu, a No. 1 draftee who didn't quite click. The addition of Brian Campbell, a touted free agent via San Jose, created headlines. But the essence of the story was this: The Blackhawks had a plan, and it didn't appear to be one of those hoary five-year plans. To wit: Marian Hossa, on the market in 2009, wanted the Blackhawks, and they wanted him, as did Hossa's fellow Red Wings free agent Tomas Kopecky. That is no trivial matter in this equation. Chicago had become a destination.

"I'm going to Chicago because I want to win a Stanley Cup," said Hossa, who did, after missing out on the silver chalice in two straight attempts the previous seasons.

But cost certainty does not confirm character, and again the Blackhawks certified their renaissance during the 2008-09 season, when they registered 46 victories and 104 points — the highest production since 1992-93, a 16-point

improvement over the previous season and 33 better than 2006-07. The buzz was back in the United Center, as were thousands more fans, some returning, many debuting.

So were playoff games on the schedule, several of them, for the first time since 2002. The young Blackhawks downed the Calgary Flames, 4-2, in the first round. In the second round, the Vancouver Canucks enjoyed a higher seed and the role of favorites, but the Blackhawks fully declared themselves as Stanley Cup contenders by continuing to exhibit an ability to play whatever style was dictated. The Blackhawks were up-tempo as was their wont; yet they also proved they could handle a physical motif. Bumping can be fun, and perhaps the Blackhawks surprised their doubters by responding to a foe possessing size and sinew.

Against world-class goalie Roberto Luongo, the Blackhawks dropped two of the first three contests. But they won Game 4 at home in OT, Game 5 in Vancouver, then Game 6 at home, 7-5, on Kane's hat trick. The Hawks had qualified for the final four. They fell to Detroit in the conference final, and a few confessed later: Maybe they had been a bit giddy, coming so far, so fast.

"But we didn't get where we want to go," concluded Sharp, clearly establishing a mantra for the next season that all would share. The Blackhawks knew they had talent, but they also knew they had a team. There is a difference. A unit had been formed, dedicated to a purpose. The Blackhawks exuded chemistry, on and off the ice. Once more, was management charmed to have put all these pieces in place? To borrow from Branch Rickey, a legendary baseball figure: Luck is the residue of design. That is, a work of art tends to stem from the art of work. ▪

[OPPOSITE] Patrick Kane (left), Andrew Ladd (right) and Patrick Sharp celebrate with goalie Antti Niemi after taking Game 6 in overtime to capture the Stanley Cup at Wachovia Center on June 9, 2010.

"I'M GOING TO CHICAGO BECAUSE I WANT TO **WIN A STANLEY CUP,"** SAID MARIAN HOSSA, WHO DID.

[ABOVE] Marian Hossa greets a crowd of young Blackhawks fans as he makes his way down the United Center stairs for his introductory press conference on July 16, 2009.

[OPPOSITE] Captain Jonathan Toews' first handoff of the Stanley Cup was to Hossa, who had lost in the Stanley Cup Final the two previous years with Pittsburgh (2008) and Detroit (2009).

BUILDING THE 2009-10 TEAM

VIA DRAFT

Bryan Bickell	Blackhawks' second-round pick, 41st overall, in the 2004 NHL Entry Draft
Dave Bolland	Blackhawks' second-round pick, 32nd overall, in the 2004 NHL Entry Draft
Troy Brouwer	Blackhawks' seventh-round pick, 214th overall, in the 2004 NHL Entry Draft
Adam Burish	Blackhawks' ninth-round pick, 282nd overall, in the 2002 NHL Entry Draft
Dustin Byfuglien	Blackhawks' eighth-round pick, 245th overall, in the 2003 NHL Entry Draft
Niklas Hjalmarsson	Blackhawks' fourth-round pick, 108th overall, in the 2005 NHL Entry Draft
Patrick Kane	Blackhawks' first-round pick, first overall, in the 2007 NHL Entry Draft
Duncan Keith	Blackhawks' second-round pick, 54th overall, in the 2002 NHL Entry Draft
Brent Seabrook	Blackhawks' first-round pick, 14th overall, in the 2003 NHL Entry Draft
Jonathan Toews	Blackhawks' first-round pick, third overall, in the 2006 NHL Entry Draft

VIA TRADE

Nick Boynton	From Anaheim in exchange for future considerations on March 2, 2010
Ben Eager	From Philadelphia in exchange for Jim Vandermeer on Dec. 18, 2007
Colin Fraser	From Philadelphia with Jim Vandermeer and a second-round pick in the 2004 NHL Entry Draft (Bryan Bickell) in exchange for Alex Zhamnov and a fourth-round pick in the 2004 NHL Entry Draft on February 19, 2004
Andrew Ladd	From Carolina in exchange for Tuomo Ruutu on February 26, 2008
Patrick Sharp	From Philadelphia with Eric Meloche in exchange for Matt Ellison and a third-round pick in the 2006 NHL Entry Draft on December 5, 2005
Kris Versteeg	From Boston in exchange for Brandon Bochenski on February 3, 2007

VIA FREE AGENCY

Brian Campbell	Signed as a free agent on July 1, 2008
Jordan Hendry	Signed as a free agent on March 18, 2006
Marian Hossa	Signed as a free agent on July 1, 2009
Cristobal Huet	Signed as a free agent on July 1, 2008
Tomas Kopecky	Signed as a free agent on July 1, 2009
John Madden	Signed as a free agent on July 2, 2009
Antti Niemi	Signed as a free agent on May 5, 2008
Brent Sopel	Signed as a free agent on September 28, 2007

[OPPOSITE] Jonathan Toews poses after the Blackhawks selected him with the third overall pick at the 2006 NHL Entry Draft.

2009-10 CHICAGO BLACKHAWKS

BRYAN BICKELL LW   29   DAVE BOLLAND C   36   NICK BOYNTON D   24   TROY BROUWER LW   22

ADAM BURISH RW   37   DUSTIN BYFUGLIEN LW   33   BRIAN CAMPBELL D   51   BEN EAGER LW   55

COLIN FRASER C   46   JORDAN HENDRY D   6   NIKLAS HJALMARSSON D   4   MARIAN HOSSA RW   81

2009-10 CHICAGO BLACKHAWKS

CRISTOBAL HUET G	39
PATRICK KANE RW	88
DUNCAN KEITH D	2
TOMAS KOPECKY C/LW	82
ANDREW LADD LW	16
JOHN MADDEN C	11
ANTTI NIEMI G	31
BRENT SEABROOK D	7
PATRICK SHARP C/LW	10
BRENT SOPEL D	5
JONATHAN TOEWS C	19
KRIS VERSTEEG LW	32

Chicago "Black Hawks"--Stanley Cup Winners, Year 1934

Emblematic of World's Professional Championship

LEFT TO RIGHT—THE LATE CHUCK GARDINER, TOMMY COOK, ROGER JENKINS, LOLA COUTURE, PAUL THOMPSON, JOHNNY GOTTSELIG, LIONEL CONACHER, ART COULTER, TOMMY GORMAN, TAFFY ABEL, DOC ROMNES, LOUIS TRUDELL, JACK LESWICK, MUSH MARSH, JOHNNY McFADDEN, BILL KENDAL, JOE STARK.

LEVINSKY

MAC KENZIE

JENKINS

MARCH

DAHLSTROM

PALANGIO

JOHNSON

KARAKAS

WᴹSTEWART
MANAGER

· STANLEY CUP ·
EMBLEMATIC
WORLD'S HOCKEY CHAMPIONSHIP

FREDERIC McLAUGHLIN
PRESIDENT

FROELICH
Trainer

GOODMAN

WᴹJ.TOBIN
VICE - PRESIDENT

CHICAGO BLACKHAWKS

WORLD'S CHAMPIONS ★ WINNERS STANLEY CUP 1937-38

COPYRIGHT CHICAGO BLACKHAWKS AND NESTOR JOHNSON SKATE CO.

THOMPSON

VOSS

SEIBERT

TRUDELL

ROMNES

WIEBE

SHILL

GOTTSELIG

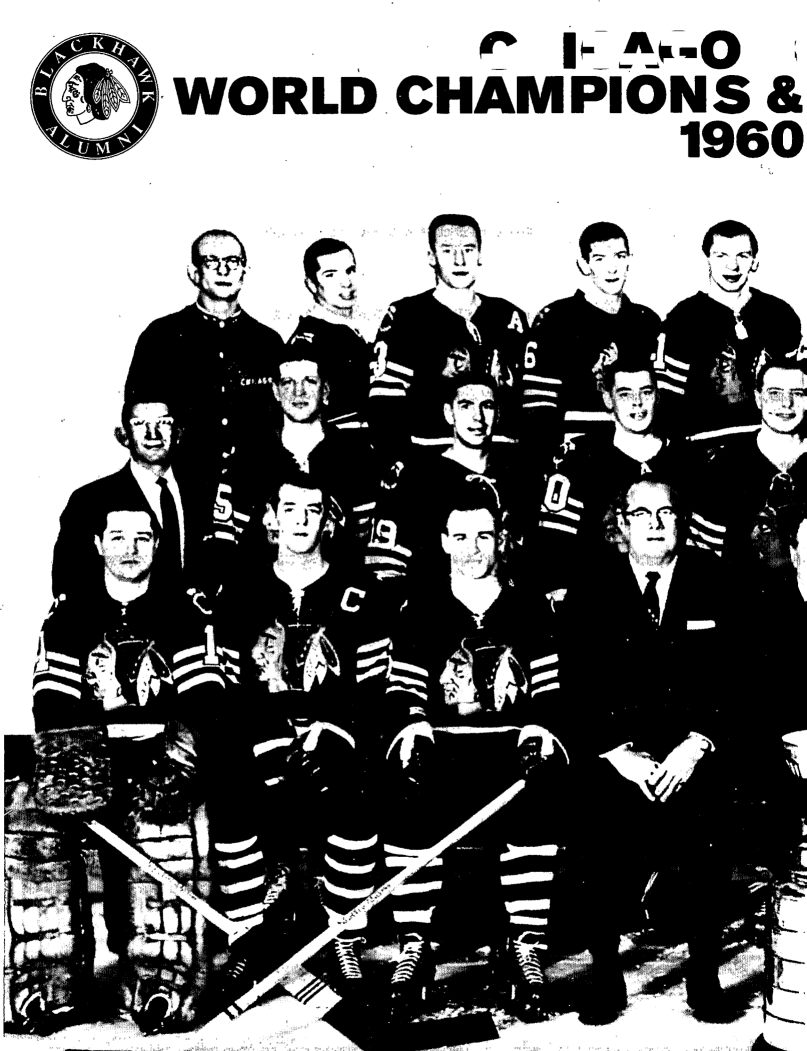

WORLD CHAMPIONS & 1960

CK HAWKS
TANLEY CUP WINNERS
1961

CHICAGO BLACKHAWKS STA

LEY CUP CHAMPIONS 2010

CHAPTER TWO
THINKING BIG

THINKING BIG

BY BOB VERDI

When the 2009-10 season opened, expectations were understandably high for the Blackhawks. So high that the organizational mantra of "One Goal" seemed less a slogan than a mission. The ideals and objectives of a progressive executive branch had been in place since October of 2007, when Rocky Wirtz assumed control of the franchise and, without so much as a pause, jump-started the process of returning this storied franchise to relevance.

You didn't need to be a Rocky scientist to discern that One Goal deserved One Gear: fast-forward. The Blackhawks were upwardly mobile the previous year, having advanced to the Western Conference Final for the first time since 1995, so anything seemed possible...

Even keeping a secret. In a wired world of sports and communications, that is no tiny task. But somehow the Blackhawks choreographed a complete surprise for the standing room audience at their United Center home debut on Saturday evening, Oct. 10. Chicago's boys of winter commenced their schedule with two games in Finland, then another in Detroit, so fans were ready and waiting for what promised to be another installment of 'the future is now'. But first, in keeping with the front office's plan on connecting history to current events, there came a rousing celebration of the past.

Bobby Hull, Stan Mikita, Tony Esposito and Denis Savard — the club's four Hall of Fame ambassadors — never had skated together. At least in public. But, in a pregame ceremony before the puck drop against the Colorado Avalanche, they appeared in uniform, one by one, from the west end of the building. Fans stood and roared for the legends, who waved their sticks as they approached center ice.

"The Golden Jet" confessed: "I can't remember the last time I laced them up, and I can't remember the last time I didn't know whether I could stop once I got going. If I hadn't gotten help from Stan and Jonathan Toews, I might still be looking for the brakes."

Credit to Blackhawks President John McDonough for conceiving this masterpiece theater idea; how the prospect of such a gala occasion remained an undercover operation is an outright mystery. After all, the four icons had "practiced" earlier in the week. And it isn't every day that "Tony O" puts on the pads.

"Since I retired," he said, "it hasn't been any day. But it felt great."

If those kids on the Blackhawks bench ever wondered what it meant to play hockey in the city of Chicago, if they ever doubted that this environment could be as special again as it once was, if they ever questioned the fervor and loyalty of this team's fan base, all they had to do on that Saturday night in October was look and listen. The current Blackhawks won the game, 4-3, when Andrew Ladd scored in the ninth round of a shootout, the longest in franchise annals.

Was there a message to be gleaned? Could these Blackhawks extend this season to its outer limits? Would there be games to be played in

[OPPOSITE] Hall of Fame ambassadors Denis Savard, Tony Esposito, Stan Mikita and Bobby Hull joined the team on the ice for the national anthem at the 2009-10 home opener.

[TOP] Patrick Sharp takes a stroll through a downtown Helsinki, Finland, park.

[ABOVE] A young fan watches the Blackhawks during their pregame skate at the NHL Premiere in Helsinki.

[OPPOSITE] Brent Seabrook (center) is mobbed by teammates Kris Versteeg (left) and Duncan Keith after scoring 26 seconds into OT to give the Blackhawks their biggest comeback victory in franchise history, a 6–5 win over the Calgary Flames, on Oct. 12, 2009.

June? Might this be the year? Anyone for omens?

Helsinki, Finland, was the dateline when the Blackhawks embarked on their 2009-10 schedule. Globalization has become part of North American professional sports. If the Cubs can open a season in Japan and the NFL can bring its Sunday fare to London, why not the NHL, which is so rich with international talent?

The Detroit Red Wings and St. Louis Blues played twice in Stockholm, Sweden, while the Blackhawks and Florida Panthers faced off in Finland. On Oct. 2, a Friday at 11 a.m. Chicago time, the season to remember commenced before 12,056 fans in Hartwall Arena. Patrick Kane registered the first goal on a dazzling breakaway, but the Blackhawks fell to Florida, 4-3, as goalie Tomas Vokoun denied Patrick Sharp on the final attempt in a shootout.

One evening later, on the subject of omens, Antti Niemi was in goal in his native land, and he recorded 21 saves toward a 4-0 victory. Niemi was voted No. 1 star of the game, after which defenseman Brian Campbell gazed into his crystal ball and remarked presciently, "Antti showed us that he is an NHL-level goalie."

October fireworks were plentiful indeed. Only two nights after the ambassadors appeared, the Blackhawks welcomed the Calgary Flames to the United Center and showed them entirely too much hospitality. On six shots in the first period, the Flames exploded to a 5-0 lead. Perhaps the Flames still were miffed about being knocked out of the previous year's playoffs by the Blackhawks. Or maybe the home team was still trying to exhale from a festive opener. Whatever, Cristobal Huet yielded three and Niemi two in relief before a stunned, restless crowd.

But the Blackhawks shocked the Flames again by rallying for a 6-5 victory, matching the greatest comeback in the NHL record book. Brent Seabrook scored the winner at 26 seconds of overtime. John Madden, Kane, Dustin Byfuglien, and Dave Bolland also tallied before Sharp deflected Duncan Keith's drive five minutes into the third to make it 5-5.

Nov. 25th was a date fans circled when the schedule came out because the Blackhawks would be visiting the powerful San Jose Sharks. The game's significance increased demonstrably when winger Marian Hossa, a world-class free agent, made his debut after undergoing shoulder surgery. Hossa excelled, scoring twice in a 7-2 romp, a mid-season statement that also was the Blackhawks' eighth straight triumph. The Blackhawks scored three shorthanded goals while mounting a 7-0 lead.

"I took a couple hits (on the shoulder), and it felt fine," Hossa said after handing the Sharks their first regulation defeat at home.

December opened with a bang when the Blackhawks downed the Columbus Blue Jackets, 4-3, at the United Center as Seabrook tallied in the 11th round of the shootout — two beyond

the short-lived franchise mark established Oct. 10. Coach Joel Quenneville lodged no complaints about working overtime, for the victory was the 500th of his career, making him just the 14th man in NHL history to reach that plateau.

"I've been a lot of great places," said Quenneville, who previously was head coach in St. Louis and Colorado over 13 seasons. "I've been fortunate, worked with good teams and great players." One of them, Hossa, registered his first goal for the Blackhawks at home.

Two days later, on Dec. 3, the Blackhawks made another declaration of purpose by signing Toews, Kane and Keith to long-term contracts, thereby underscoring General Manager Stan Bowman's intentions to retain core players.

"When I took this job last summer," said Bowman, "my first two calls were to Pat Brisson, who handles Patrick and Jonathan, and Ross Gurney, who represents Duncan. I wanted to get those three key guys locked up as soon as possible.

A COROLLARY ABOUT COMMITMENT: HOW MANY FRANCHISES POSSESS THREE SUCH TALENTS WORTH THE EFFORT?

[ABOVE] On Dec. 3, 2009, the Blackhawks announced contract extensions for stars Jonathan Toews (left), Patrick Kane (center) and Duncan Keith, who stopped by WGN Radio's studios following their press conference.
[OPPOSITE] Coach Joel Quenneville lays out the Hawks strategy prior to facing Phoenix on the team's Father-Son Trip.

Everybody was on board, and it still took several months to get done."

Captain Toews and Kane, two gifted forwards, each were extended by five years while Keith agreed to a 13-year deal. Management distinguished itself by being proactive in securing three young stars despite the tight confines of the NHL hard salary cap. A corollary about commitment: How many sports franchises possess three such talents worth the effort?

In January, NBC initiated its schedule of national weekend telecasts, and the network did not err in choosing the visceral rivalry between the Blackhawks and Red Wings. On the third Sunday afternoon of 2010, a terrific intra-division match resulted in a 4-3 conquest for the Hawks, who lost leads of 2-0 and 3-2 before Sharp scored the clincher in a dramatic shootout. Hossa was booed emphatically in his return to Joe Louis Arena, but he also tallied during the shootout while Niemi made 35 saves toward the Blackhawks' third consecutive decision over the Red Wings, who had been blanked in the previous two.

February's Olympic break was anything but for six Blackhawks who participated in the Winter Games at Vancouver. A sterling competition resulted in a classic matchup: United States vs. Canada on Sunday afternoon the 28th, and the game exceeded expectations, especially for the home team that authored a pressurized 3-2 win on an overtime goal by Pittsburgh's Sidney Crosby.

Even Toews, whose all-around performance earned him the title of outstanding forward for the entire tournament, thought it appropriate that Crosby brought Canada a gold medal with virtually the whole country on pins and needles.

Seabrook and Keith, a stalwart on defense for Canada, celebrated the triumph while Kane earned a silver medal for the gritty Americans, who forged a 2-2 deadlock with just 24 seconds remaining in regulation.

"Pretty scary when, at that point, it's anybody's game in OT," reflected Toews, who scored earlier. "But we had to believe in ourselves all the way, and it's unbelievable, wearing this gold medal around my neck. It's really hard to grasp how big it really is. You are in this one building, and you can't even understand how many people

[OPPOSITE] Canadians Brent Seabrook (left), Jonathan Toews (center) and Duncan Keith took gold in the 2010 Winter Olympics, beating teammate Patrick Kane and Team USA in overtime 3-2.

Six Blackhawks represented their countries during the 2010 Winter Olympics in Vancouver. From left to right: Tomas Kopecky and Marian Hossa (Slovakia); Patrick Kane (United States); and Jonathan Toews, Brent Seabrook and Duncan Keith (Canada).

"I REMEMBER THE FEELING WE HAD IN 1961," SAID BOBBY HULL. "I'VE GOT THE SAME FEELING ABOUT THIS BUNCH. I REALLY DO. WHY NOT THINK BIG?"

watched this and how it affects them."

Hossa and Tomas Kopecky played for Team Slovakia. The Blackhawks were scheduled to resume the NHL regular season two nights later on Long Island, so Rocky Wirtz struck again. He arranged a charter flight for his athletes to the East Coast, a gesture that did not go unnoticed. "It was much appreciated," said Seabrook.

On April 4, the Blackhawks celebrated Easter Sunday at the United Center by clinching the Central Division title, their first since they won the Norris Division in 1993. With all those Olympians enduring the grind in Vancouver, fans were apprehensive about possible after effects. But the Blackhawks professed certain goals in October, and this one actually was confirmed by way of Philadelphia, where the Flyers defeated the surging Red Wings earlier in the afternoon. Still, the Blackhawks polished off Calgary, 4-1.

"It's been a long time coming," noted Kane, who scored along with Kopecky, Brouwer and Byfuglien. "I was four the last time we won the division. It's a good accomplishment, but it's not really the accomplishment you want."

Two nights later in Dallas, the Blackhawks whipped the Stars, 5-2, for their 50th victory — a franchise record. Hossa tallied 36 seconds into the first period, and Colin Fraser bagged his first of two in the final minute of the same session. In two previous seasons — 1970-71 and 1990-91 — the Blackhawks had amassed 49 wins. There were ties in those days, true, and points were more scarce, but the benchmark in Dallas constituted another building block, albeit not the last one.

By season's end the Blackhawks had accumulated 52 victories, the highest point total in team history (112) and the best record on the road, 23 wins.

Surely, when reviewing highlights of the 2009-10 season, honorable mentions abound. In early December the Blackhawks went to Pittsburgh and beat the defending Stanley Cup champion Penguins, 2-1, on Kris Versteeg's overtime goal. In March Vancouver visited the United Center on an electric Friday night, and the Blackhawks strafed Roberto Luongo, Canada's gold medal goalie, for five first-period goals in a 6-3 frolic.

During late March the Blackhawks were in a rough patch when the rampaging Phoenix Coyotes came to the United Center on a nine-game winning streak with an eye on first place in the Western Conference. But the Blackhawks prevailed behind Niemi, 2-0, and Quenneville called it the biggest game of the year while hoping that there would be another biggest game of the year, maybe several.

You can look it up — on opening night in October, after he finally screeched to a halt, Bobby Hull went back to his seat, shedding his uniform and skates, but not his enthusiasm.

"I remember the feeling we had in 1961," said Hull. "I was a kid, like a lot of kids on this current team. But on the Blackhawks then, we just had a notion we were going places. I've got that same feeling about this bunch. I really do. Why not think big?" ▨

[OPPOSITE] Coach Joel Quenneville and the Blackhawks bench before a game against Dallas in February.

VIEW FROM THE BOOTH

WITH EDDIE OLCZYK: 2010 WINTER OLYMPICS GOLD MEDAL GAME

From an excitement level the first U.S.-Canada matchup (Feb. 21, 2010) was unbelievable – just with the atmosphere and all the back and forth scoring. But it was a play-in game; you were going to live to fight another day regardless of who won. When you get to a championship game, it's different. You're not going to be as loose; you're not going to let things go.

Going into the gold medal game, I felt that all the pressure was on Canada. That win earlier in the tournament for the U.S. put some doubt in the Canadians' minds. If the U.S. could hang around, they would get what they wanted. And at times the U.S. did hang in there. Roberto Luongo was very tentative in the net, but the Canadians did a great job of holding onto the puck and not giving up opportunities. Then all of a sudden the U.S. started coming on, and they were getting chances. The Canadians were on their heels, and obviously the rest is history.

I don't think there's any doubt that the two best defensemen for Canada were Duncan Keith and Drew Doughty (Los Angeles Kings). With more ice time comes more opportunity, and Dunc took advantage of that. Whether it was earning more power play time, being out there as one of the top four or killing penalties, he earned it. His confidence and positioning were killer. He was reliable and played an integral part in securing Canada's gold medal. When I think about everything that took place — gold medal, Stanley Cup and Norris Trophy — it was a hell of a year for him.

Talking to Canadian head coach Mike Babcock before the tournament and watching how he used Jonathan Toews from start to the finish, I think he knew Johnny was a flexible player who could take on any situation. As the tournament went on, his role got bigger, he became better, and everybody got a chance to see the type of player he is at the highest stage. I think Babcock was looking for him to fill a certain role, but it expanded, and he played in every situation. As his role evolved, he became a difference maker for Canada.

Brent Seabrook's role was limited at the Olympics, but regardless of how many minutes he played, just to be on that team out of some 80 other defensemen the Canadians could have taken speaks volumes about his character and talent. Looking back on Game 6 of the Stanley Cup Final in Philadelphia, that was Seabrook's best game as a pro, and I'm sure the Olympic experience was immensely valuable for him.

This Olympics was a changing of the guard, especially for Team USA. It was a younger team with different dynamics. As the tournament went on, Patrick Kane got better and better. When the game was on the line or they needed a big win — whether it was the Finland game or tying it up to force overtime against the Canadians in the gold medal game — Kaner was there.

I don't think there's any doubt that the Olympic experience helps players in future endeavors. Any time you can compete at the highest level, those high-fevered games help you the next time around. It's not necessarily physical, but mental, especially for the young guys.

The impact of the Blackhawks players for their respective countries was amazing really. I think the Olympic experience certainly wet their whistles for what was to come.

— Television color analyst Eddie Olczyk provided commentary for NBC at the 2010 Winter Olympics

TEAM BONDING: FUN IN THE SUN

BY ANNE E. STEIN

Whether it was hanging out on hotel couches with Mario Kart steering wheels in hand or boarding a boat for Alcatraz to tour the infamous prison, the 2009-10 Chicago Blackhawks spent an enormous amount of time together on and off the ice, developing into one of the tightest teams in the NHL.

"In my 11 years here, I don't think I've seen a group that's any closer," says Tony Ommen, senior director, team services, who coordinates travel, meals, hotels and other day-to-day activity for the team. "Everybody really seems to like each other and get along."

The on-ice chemistry was obvious, starting with the offensive pairing of Jonathan Toews and Patrick Kane and the defensive duo of Brent Seabrook and Duncan Keith. When things needed to be mixed up a bit — because no matter how much you like someone, it's good to get an occasional break — coach Joel Quenneville scrambled his lines to come up with some hockey magic.

Off the ice the chemistry clicked as well. These 24 guys hung out together, at home and on the road. In Chicago they'd carpool to practices and share lunches and dinners. Most pro athletes get dressed and scatter quickly after practices and games; the Hawks would linger long after mid-morning practice at the United Center, joking and enjoying each other's company.

While the boys bonded on their own, the team made things official with an early-season father-son road trip. Hawks players and management, along with several of their dads and a few granddads and brothers, traveled west in November to Phoenix and Denver. They played golf together in Phoenix and enjoyed a post-tournament banquet. The guests watched practices and games, and as a surprise to the fathers and players, got to sit in the locker room with their sons as Coach Q went over pregame x's and o's. The trip was so successful that a Mother-Son Trip is in the plans for 2010-11.

Other season highlights together included the team's March 16 visit to "The Tonight Show with Jay Leno" on their road trip to Los Angeles and Anaheim. Seated in two long rows, Patrick Kane got the dialogue going with a comedy bit involving his silver medal shining in Jay's eyes. After audience applause for Kane, Toews stood up to point out his, Seabrook and Keith's superior gold medals for Team Canada. Later the Olympians got a shout-out from guest Hugh Jackman.

[TOP] Patrick Kane (right) makes a putt during the Father-Son Trip golf outing.
[ABOVE] Brian Campbell and his father, Ed, at the Hawks' Phoenix resort.
[OPPOSITE] Kane and Patrick Sharp goof around before practice.

[TOP] Kris Versteeg (left) and Andrew Ladd have a bite to eat at the Palace Grill Restaurant after a December practice. The guys bought lunch for patrons and shot a Blackhawks TV segment.

[ABOVE] The Blackhawks prepare for a morning skate in Phoenix.

[OPPOSITE] Patrick Kane (left) and John Madden joke while getting ready for a morning skate prior to a game against Phoenix in November.

[TOP] Television play-by-play announcer Pat Foley (right) plays talk show host to Executive Vice President Jay Blunk (center) and Vice President/Assistant to the President Al MacIsaac on the set of "The Tonight Show with Jay Leno."

[ABOVE] The Blackhawks pose for a photo with Jay Leno following their late-night debut.

[OPPOSITE TOP] With a makeshift microphone, Patrick Kane (left) "interviews" Brian Campbell during Blackhawks TV's speed skating mini-Olympic event.

[OPPOSITE BOTTOM LEFT] Tomas Kopecky tapes up his stick before a road practice.

[OPPOSITE BOTTOM RIGHT] From left to right: Ben Eager, Jonathan Toews and Kris Versteeg head to the bus to go to the practice rink in Anaheim.

DEFINING MOMENT

BY TIM SASSONE

As far back as November, the Blackhawks had the look of a Stanley Cup champion, goaltending issues and all. There wasn't another team in the NHL that could match the depth of the Hawks, who won their first championship in 49 years largely with coach Joel Quenneville rolling four lines on a regular basis.

The Hawks were 8-5-2 in early November when they went on an eight-game winning streak that started their separation from the pack in the Western Conference. The eighth win was especially significant in that it marked the debut of Marian Hossa, the Hawks' prized free-agent signing from the summer of 2009.

Hossa scored two goals in his first game with the Hawks, a 7-2 drubbing of the San Jose Sharks at HP Pavilion. His presence on the ice and in the dressing room took the Hawks to another level in terms of scoring depth and veteran influence. Hossa not only gave the Hawks another top-end scoring threat to go with Jonathan Toews, Patrick Kane and Patrick Sharp, but his veteran leadership, professionalism and underrated play on the defensive side of the puck was a revelation to those who never had the chance to watch him play in Atlanta, Ottawa, Pittsburgh or Detroit.

From the night Hossa returned from offseason shoulder surgery on Nov. 25 at San Jose through the end of February, the Hawks went 26-10-3, capturing 55 out of a possible 78 points.

Hossa also was a difference maker in the playoffs, even though he didn't exactly light it up offensively with three goals in 22 games. But he did have 12 assists and scored one of the three biggest goals of the postseason for the Hawks — the other two being Kane's Cup-clincher in overtime in Game 6 in Philadelphia and Kane's late shorthanded goal that tied Game 5 against Nashville in the first round.

Hossa's overtime goal in that same Game 5 against the Predators at the United Center saved the opening round for the Hawks and gave them the lift they needed at that time to believe they could go all the way. After winning the Stanley Cup, many of the Hawks spoke of Hossa's Game 5 overtime goal in special terms.

"That goal right there won us the Stanley Cup," Hawks winger Kris Versteeg said. "We just carried off that every day after that."

A loss in Game 5 would have sent the Hawks back to Nashville down 3-2 in the series, but Hossa changed everything on that memorable Sunday afternoon in April when he scored moments after exiting the penalty box.

"A dramatic turn of events," Quenneville said. "There are defining moments in each and every series."

Without Hossa's goal Toews and Dustin Byfuglien might not have had the chance to star in the second round against Vancouver; Antti Niemi might not have had the opportunity to star in the conference final against San Jose; and there might not have been Kane's Game 6 heroics on that June night in Philadelphia.

— Tim Sassone has covered the Blackhawks and the NHL for the Daily Herald since 1988

FROM THE NIGHT HOSSA RETURNED FROM OFFSEASON SHOULDER SURGERY THROUGH THE END OF FEBRUARY, THE HAWKS WENT 26-10-3, CAPTURING 55 OUT OF A POSSIBLE 78 POINTS.

BY SEASON'S END THE BLACKHAWKS HAD ACCUMULATED 52 VICTORIES, THE HIGHEST POINT TOTAL IN TEAM HISTORY (112) AND THE BEST RECORD ON THE ROAD, 23 WINS.

JONATHAN TOEWS 19
Forward CHICAGO BLACKHAWKS

1934 ★ 1938   STANLEY CUP CHAMPIONS   1961 ★ 2010

2009-10 REGULAR SEASON

PLAYER	POS	GP	G	A	P	+/-	PIM	PP	SH	GW	S	S%	TOI/G
Patrick Kane	R	82	30	58	88	16	20	9	0	6	261	11.5	19:11
Duncan Keith	D	82	14	55	69	21	51	3	1	1	213	6.6	26:35
Jonathan Toews	C	76	25	43	68	22	47	9	1	3	202	12.4	20:00
Patrick Sharp	L/C	82	25	41	66	24	28	4	2	4	266	9.4	18:07
Marian Hossa	R	57	24	27	51	24	18	2	5	2	199	12.1	18:43
Kris Versteeg	L	79	20	24	44	8	35	4	3	4	184	10.9	15:43
Troy Brouwer	R	78	22	18	40	9	66	7	1	7	116	19.0	16:22
Andrew Ladd	L	82	17	21	38	2	67	0	0	1	148	11.5	13:41
Brian Campbell	D	68	7	31	38	18	18	3	0	2	131	5.3	23:12
Dustin Byfuglien	R	82	17	17	34	-7	94	6	0	3	211	8.1	16:25
Brent Seabrook	D	78	4	26	30	20	59	0	0	2	129	3.1	23:13
John Madden	C	79	10	13	23	-2	12	0	0	0	127	7.9	15:24
Tomas Kopecky	R	74	10	11	21	0	28	1	0	2	95	10.5	9:28
Colin Fraser	C	70	7	12	19	6	44	0	0	0	92	7.6	9:35
Niklas Hjalmarsson	D	77	2	15	17	9	20	0	0	1	62	3.2	19:39
Ben Eager	L	60	7	9	16	9	120	0	0	2	68	10.3	8:19
Dave Bolland	C	39	6	10	16	5	28	1	0	0	52	11.5	17:21
Cam Barker	D	51	4	10	14	7	58	3	0	1	74	5.4	13:05
Jordan Hendry	D	43	2	6	8	5	10	0	0	1	42	4.8	11:51
Brent Sopel	D	73	1	7	8	3	34	0	0	0	48	2.1	14:51
Bryan Bickell	L	16	3	1	4	4	5	0	0	1	20	15.0	9:35
Adam Burish	R	13	1	3	4	2	14	0	0	0	9	11.1	8:46
Kim Johnsson	D	8	1	2	3	7	4	0	0	0	10	10.0	16:24
Jack Skille	R	6	1	1	2	-3	0	0	0	0	9	11.1	7:39
Jake Dowell	C	3	1	1	2	1	5	0	0	0	4	25.0	6:56
Andrew Ebbett	C	10	1	0	1	1	2	0	0	0	14	7.1	10:43
Nick Boynton	D	7	0	1	1	4	12	0	0	0	11	0.0	15:56
Radek Smolenak	L	1	0	0	0	0	5	0	0	0	1	0.0	4:41

GOALTENDER	GP	MINS	AVG	W	L	OT	EN	SO	GA	SA	SV%	G	A	PIM
Antti Niemi	39	2,190:28	2.25	26	7	4	-	7	82	936	.912	0	1	0
Cristobal Huet	48	2,731:14	2.50	26	14	4	-	4	114	1083	.895	0	0	4
Corey Crawford	1	59:13	3.05	0	1	0	-	0	3	35	.914	0	0	0

CHAPTER THREE
THE QUEST BEGINS

BRE-W()A)

CHICAGO BLACKHAWKS 2009-10

W. ROCKWELL WIRTZ JOHN MCDONOUGH JAY BLUNK
STAN BOWMAN AL MACISAAC KEVIN CHEVELDAYOFF SCOTTY BOWMAN
DALE TALLON JOEL QUENNEVILLE MIKE HAVILAND
JOHN TORCHETTI STEPHANE WAITE MIKE GAPSKI TROY PARCHMAN
JEFF THOMAS CLINT REIF PAWEL PRYLINSKI JIM HEINTZELMAN
PAUL GOODMAN PAUL VINCENT BRAD ALDRICH MARC BERGEVIN
MARK KELLEY NORM MACIVER MICHEL DUMAS RON ANDERSON
TONY OMMEN MARK BERNARD DR. MICHAEL TERRY
JONATHAN TOEWS CAPT. DAVE BOLLAND NICK BOYNTON

T he Stanley Cup Playoffs. There is nothing like it in professional sports. To earn that cherished 35-pound silver mug, a team must win 16 postseason games over four best-of-seven series that consume two months. When the Blackhawks concluded their regular schedule on April 11, they had only that number in mind —16 — and no plans to play golf, go fishing or return to their summer residences until late June. Easier said than done.

Western Conference Quarterfinals

The Nashville Predators are like your in-laws. You haven't seen them since Christmas, and you haven't thought about them much, so you forget how annoying they can be. The Blackhawks received a quick, bracing refresher course with a 4-1 loss in the opener at the United Center. Anyone paying attention to the regular season would not have been shocked. True, the Predators were a No. 7 seed, but they amassed 100 points, won only five fewer games than the Blackhawks and matched Chicago with 23 road victories.

The Blackhawks tied the series with a 2-0 triumph in Game 2 behind Antti Niemi, who registered the team's first postseason shutout since Ed Belfour in 1996. But the Blackhawks bowed in Game 3 at Nashville, 4-1, and the Predators smelled an upset. In Game 4, Brian Campbell re-entered the lineup after incurring a serious shoulder injury in mid-March, and the Blackhawks won, 3-0, as Niemi joined Tony Esposito, who recorded two playoff shutouts in the same series in 1974.

Game 5 found the Blackhawks in serious trouble. They trailed, 4-3, in a Saturday afternoon national telecast. They not only trailed, they trailed late. Then, with 1:03 remaining in

regulation, Marian Hossa drew a five-minute major penalty. All the feisty Predators had to do was hang on for their second series victory at the United Center, then go home to try for the clincher and a huge upset. But Nashville committed a turnover in its own zone, and Patrick Kane scored a shorthanded goal with 13.6 seconds left in the third period to forge a 4-4 tie. In overtime, only 11 seconds after serving his time, Hossa tallied from close range against goalie Pekka Rinne. Hossa went to his knees, and the crowd went wild, hailing the 5-4 conquest by showering the ice with red playoff towels that were intended to be kept as souvenirs.

"Unbelievable," gushed Kane. Concluded coach Joel Quenneville: "It was a little bit too dramatic for me, but we like the result."

The Blackhawks eliminated Nashville, 5-3, to win the series, 4 games to 2, but Game 6 was not easy. The visiting Blackhawks jumped to a 3-1 lead but were tied, 3-3, during a frantic first period. Jonathan Toews registered the winner on a power play, and Niemi survived a tense third period, recording 13 saves. "That's a good hockey team we just beat," said defenseman Brent Sopel, who blocked 19 shots in the series.

GAME ONE

APRIL 16, 2010

Though the Blackhawks and their 22,256 fans were excited for the return of playoff hockey to the United Center, it was the Nashville Predators who did most of the celebrating. After falling behind 1-0 on a goal from Patrick Kane, the Predators notched four third period goals (two by former Hawk J.P. Dumont) to record their first road playoff victory in franchise history.

[TOP] Patrick Sharp (left) and Patrick Kane celebrate after Kane's wrister in the second put the Hawks ahead 1–0.
[ABOVE LEFT] Carlos Marmol, Marlon Byrd (front) and the entire Chicago Cubs team took in Game 1 at the United Center.
[ABOVE RIGHT] Duncan Keith dives for the puck in the Hawks' 4–1 loss to Nashville in the first round of the Western Conference Quarterfinals.
[OPPOSITE] An enthusiastic fan sings along with Jim Cornelison's stirring rendition of the national anthem.

GAME TWO

APRIL 18, 2010

After losing their playoff opener to the Nashville Predators, 4-1, at the United Center, the Blackhawks rebounded with a 2-0 victory. Antti Niemi made 23 saves to record the first postseason shutout for the team since Ed Belfour in 1996. Dave Bolland and Patrick Kane scored against the pesky, disciplined visitors. The Blackhawks killed all five penalties.

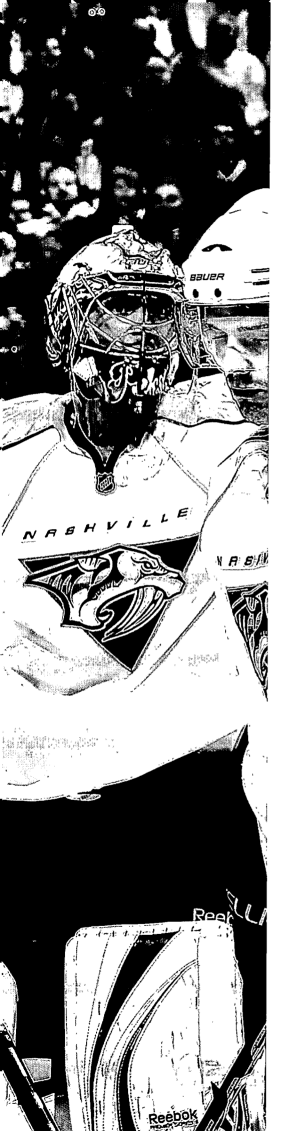

[TOP] Members of the Chicago White Sox watched Game 2. Top row, from left to right: A.J. Pierzynski, Jake Peavy, Donny Lucy and John Danks. Bottom row, from left to right: Paul Konerko, Jayson Nix and Gordon Beckham.

[ABOVE] Goalie Antti Niemi and Duncan Keith team up to stop Nashville's Colin Wilson.

[OPPOSITE] Patrick Kane and Dave Bolland react in disbelief after the referees call no goal. Each would score later in the game.

Western Conference Quarterfinals

GAME THREE
APRIL 20, 2010

Playing before a Bridgestone Arena crowd of 16,075, the Blackhawks dropped Game 3 in Nashville, giving the Predators a 2-1 series lead. The Hawks could only sneak one past Pekka Rinne, tying it up in the first with a backhander from Tomas Kopecky. David Legwand's goal and two assists, coupled with Martin Erat's penalty-shot goal, lifted Nashville to the 4-1 victory.

[ABOVE] Tomas Kopecky celebrates his first period goal in Game 3 at Bridgestone Arena.
[OPPOSITE TOP] Nashville's Joel Ward tries to sneak the puck past Antti Niemi and Dustin Byfuglien.
[OPPOSITE BOTTOM] Colin Fraser takes a big hit during the third period.

GAME FOUR
APRIL 22, 2010

Again the Blackhawks were forced to respond following a 4-1 defeat in Nashville, and they did so, again behind Antti Niemi. The netminder faced 33 shots as the Blackhawks prevailed, 3-0, to tie the best-of-seven series, 2-2. Niemi became the first Chicago goalie to record two shutouts in a playoff series since Tony Esposito in 1974, and Patrick Sharp tallied twice.

[TOP] Jonathan Toews scores with 7:05 left in the second to make it 2–0 Hawks.
[ABOVE LEFT] Patrick Kane looks to move the puck out of the Blackhawks' zone.
[ABOVE RIGHT] Antti Niemi registered his second shutout of the postseason in Game 4.
[OPPOSITE] Patrick Sharp beat Predators netminder Pekka Rinne twice in the Hawks' win.

GAME FIVE

APRIL 24, 2010

The Blackhawks downed Nashville, 6-5, in overtime of Game 5, an afternoon often cited as a defining moment in their march toward a Stanley Cup. The Hawks trailed, 4-3, when Marian Hossa incurred a five-minute major penalty with 1:03 left in regulation. The Predators were that close to taking a 3-2 series lead back home, but Patrick Kane tallied shorthanded with just 13.6 seconds left, and Hossa redeemed himself with the overtime winner.

[TOP LEFT] Patrick Kane celebrates the Game 5 victory as fans shower the ice with souvenir playoff towels.
[TOP RIGHT] Tomas Kopecky (left) and Jonathan Toews played key roles in the Hawks' all-important 6-5 win over Nashville.
[ABOVE & OPPOSITE] After taking a major penalty, Marian Hossa came out of the box to score the dramatic, game-winning goal.

DEFINING MOMENT

BY ADAM L. JAHNS

Patrick Kane said it was "indescribable and unbelievable" and coach Joel Quenneville summarized the finish as "pretty remarkable."

Game 5 of the Blackhawks' first-round series against the Nashville Predators was certainly many things. It was arguably the most exciting game of the entire postseason for the Stanley Cup-winning Hawks. Looking back now, it also was the most important.

The Hawks' dramatic, come-from-behind 5-4 win in overtime transformed Stanley Cup aspirations into Cup-hoisting anticipation. The Hawks displayed a remarkable resilience in Game 5 that showed up throughout the remainder of the postseason.

The Hawks went from possibly looking up from a 3-2 series deficit to taking a 3-2 series lead in a matter of seconds. Kane's shorthanded goal with 13.6 seconds remaining in regulation forced overtime, and Marian Hossa netted the game-winner at 4:07 in the extra period — 11 seconds after he left the penalty box following a five-minute major boarding penalty.

Just imagine if the Hawks had not rallied and Nashville had prevailed. The Hawks had a two-goal advantage in Game 5, which quickly disappeared at the hands of the Predators. Momentum had been a difficult thing to hold on to throughout the series, but Nashville would have undoubtedly had all of it with Game 6 in their own building if they'd held off the Hawks.

Put it this way: The Hawks were just 13 seconds away from heading down a path that could have led to their 49-year drought ballooning into one spanning half a century.

The Hawks penalty-killers were remarkable in Game 5, and the remarkable things kept coming. The bounces continued to go their way in Game 6 and so on. You need not look any farther than Brent Seabrook's attempted dump-in, which ricocheted off Kane and into an empty goal — Predators goalie Pekka Rinne had moved to play the puck — to give the Hawks the lead in Game 6 as a prime example.

The Hawks won Game 6 in Nashville and took the series. They then looked dominant against the Vancouver Canucks in the second round, swept the San Jose Sharks in the Western Conference Final and overcame another resilient opponent in the Philadelphia Flyers to take home the Stanley Cup.

FROM GAME 5 AGAINST NASHVILLE ON, YOU BELIEVED THAT THE HAWKS WOULD FIND A WAY TO WIN ANY GAME AND ANY SERIES.

It's important to remember that the Hawks were considered contenders from Day 1. A run at the Stanley Cup was expected. It was their unexpected run to the Western Conference Final a year earlier that increased those expectations. They were fast, tough, deep and confident. Everyone wanted more from the Hawks, especially themselves.

But the speed bumps the Hawks ran into against the Predators — a 100-point team during the regular season — raised questions about their confidence and experience. The Predators had a 2-1 series lead, and it started to look as if all the expectations were simply too much for one of the youngest teams in the NHL to handle.

Nashville had executed their trap to near perfection at times. They slowed down the Hawks' quick transition game, clogged passing lanes and took advantage of mistakes. The Predators were even finding success with one of their best players, Patric Hornqvist, out of the lineup. That success also forced Brian Campbell to return from his injuries — a broken rib and collarbone — earlier than expected.

Still, there always was an uncanny calmness in the Hawks locker room. They were simply a confident group. Any doubts developing on the outside never crept inside. For the Hawks it always had been about what they didn't do, not what their opponents were able to do against them. When they needed to, the Hawks could flip the switch, skate, score and win.

From Game 5 against Nashville on, you believed that the Hawks would find a way to win any game and any series. That when push came to shove — when the Canucks came in and embarrassed the Hawks in Game 5 and when the Flyers rallied to even the best-of-seven Cup series — the Hawks would respond and prevail.

And they did. Every time.

— Adam L. Jahns covers the Blackhawks for the Chicago Sun-Times

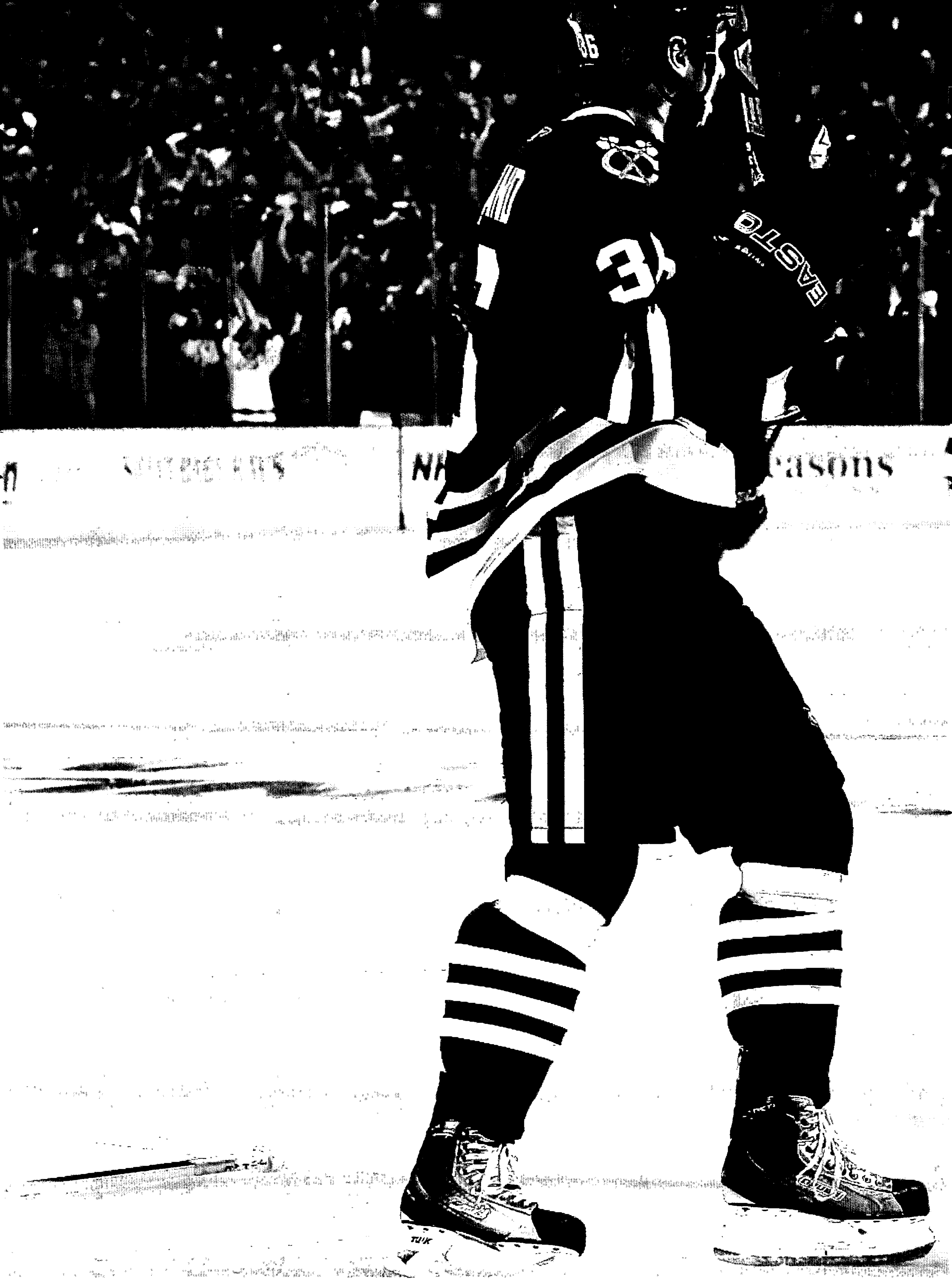

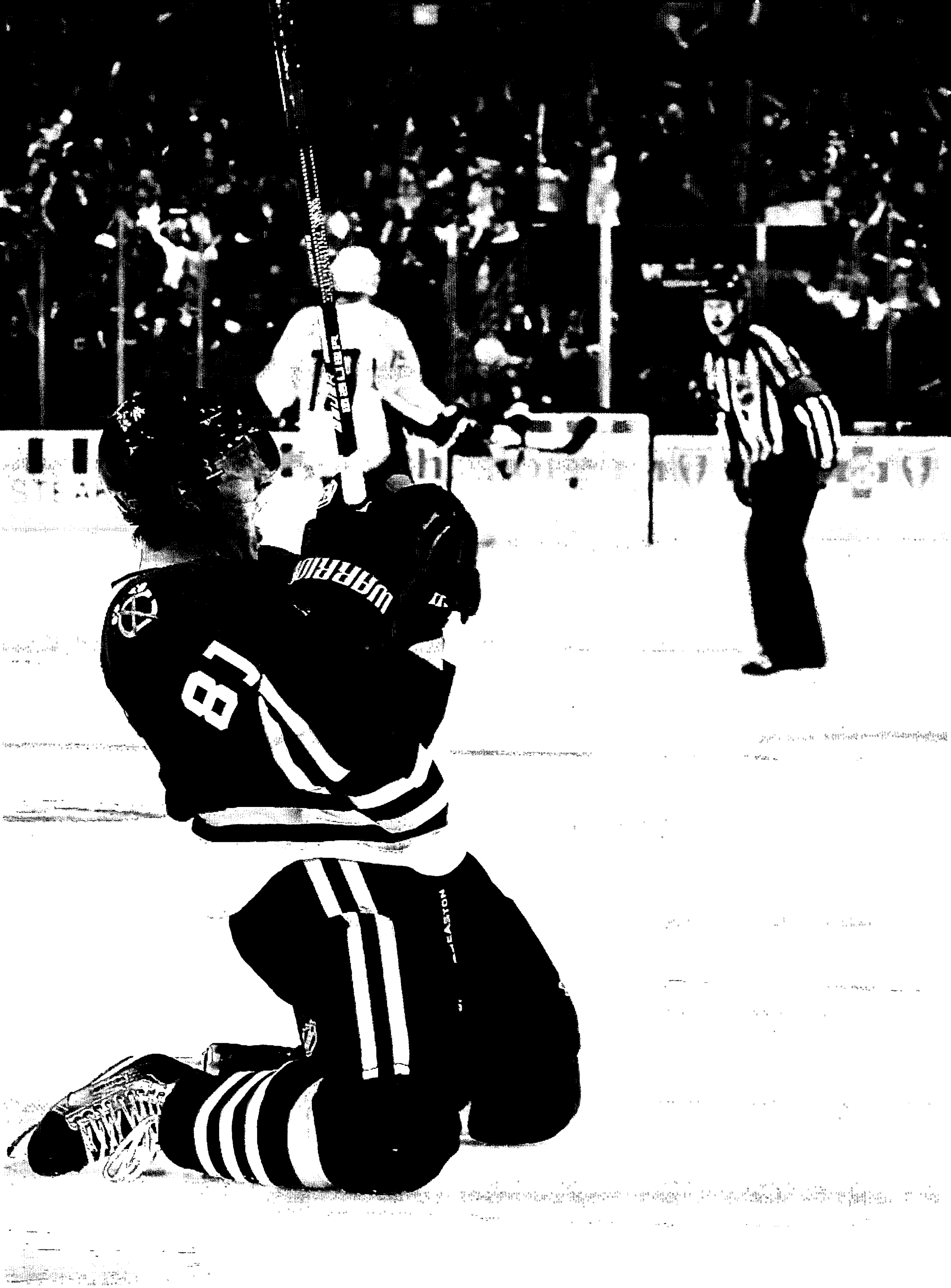
EASTON

GAME SIX
APRIL 26, 2010

The Blackhawks eliminated the Predators, 5-3, to win the series, 4 games to 2, and advance to the second round. The Blackhawks surged to a 3-1 lead during a wild first period. The Predators rallied to tie on two goals by Jason Arnott, but Jonathan Toews regained the lead on a power play for a 4-3 advantage. The game settled down thereafter, although Antti Niemi was tested in the final period when he registered 13 saves.

[TOP] Patrick Sharp celebrates one of his three Game 6 points.
[ABOVE LEFT] The Blackhawks bench reacts after an empty-net goal sealed the series.
[ABOVE RIGHT] Hawks captain Jonathan Toews congratulates Nashville goalie Pekka Rinne on a tough-fought series.
[OPPOSITE] The Hawks defeated the Predators to win the series 4 games to 2 and advance to the Western Conference Semifinals.

Western Conference Semifinals

The Vancouver Canucks, ousted by the Blackhawks in the 2009 playoffs, stormed into the United Center in a vengeful mood and eased to a 5-1 Game 1 victory. Roberto Luongo stopped 17 shots in the first period, and the Canucks dominated. The visitors then took a 2-0 lead in Game 2, and the Blackhawks appeared to be out of sync until Brent Seabrook scored on their first shot on Luongo. The Blackhawks settled down, then mounted an important third period rally that included a clutch shorthanded goal by Patrick Sharp to tie it, 2-2, and Kris Versteeg's winner at 18:30. Kane's empty-net tally achieved the 4-3 final, but Toews was not speaking for only himself when he stated afterward, "That was definitely not the start we wanted."

General Motors Place was loud for Game 3, at least for a while. Then Dustin Byfuglien established a visitor's residence near Luongo and converted three rebounds, two on power plays, for a hat trick that led the Blackhawks to a 5-2 decision. The series developed more of an edge as players jawed and bumped.

The third period closed with a flurry of misconduct penalties, but Byfuglien's silencers had served their purpose, even if Vancouver coach Alain Vigneault experienced difficulty in pronouncing the big forward's name. After the contest, "Big Buff" was asked whether the Canucks might discover a solution for his ability to hang out on Luongo's doorstep. Said Byfuglien: "I don't think so."

The Canucks tried to dislodge Byfuglien, and as much as said so before Game 4. We have to fight fire with fire, promised Vigneault. Meanwhile Toews went on a binge by becoming the first Blackhawk to garner three power-play goals in a playoff game, and Chicago's road warriors roared to a 7-4 conquest and a 3-1 lead in the series, much to the dismay of Canuck fans. Captain Hat Trick also added two assists as the Blackhawks established momentum at the 18 second mark when Seabrook scored through the five-hole on Luongo, who rued afterward, "We lost our composure tonight."

The Canucks rebounded with a 4-1 triumph in Game 5 at the United Center, but the Blackhawks declined to lean on the possibility that they still could win the series there in Game 7. Instead they gladly packed for nine days on the road, and all that clean laundry came in handy after the Blackhawks waxed Vancouver, 5-1, in Game 6 at General Motors Place to win the series — on May 11, the exact date when the vanquished Canucks shaved their playoff beards a year ago. The Canucks were nonplussed. Vancouver had won an NHL best 30 games at home during the regular season but dropped three straight there to the Blackhawks.

Vancouver fantasized about a Stanley Cup as a nice bookend to Canada's gold medal at the February Winter Olympics there, but the Blackhawks had other ideas and perpetrated their own version of a closing ceremony in Vancouver. They were off to San Jose, with a copious amount of clothes and confidence.

GAME ONE
MAY 1, 2010

It's not easy to turn a sold-out United Center crowd silent, but the Canucks managed to do just that in Game 1 of the Western Conference Semifinals. Hawks goalie Antti Niemi was overwhelmed by a Vancouver blitz that pushed the Canucks up five goals in just less than 23 minutes of play. He was pulled in favor of Cristobal Huet in the third period. Vancouver goaltender Roberto Luongo made 36 saves, keeping the Hawks to just one goal.

[TOP] The United Center comes alive as the Blackhawks take on the Canucks in Game 1 of the Western Conference Semifinals.
[ABOVE] Jonathan Toews (left) fights through the Canucks defense for a shot at the net.
[OPPOSITE] Tomas Kopecky and Kris Versteeg (right) get physical with the Canucks during Game 1.

GAME TWO

MAY 3, 2010

Game 2 didn't get off to an ideal start as the Canucks pulled ahead 2-0 early in the first period, but the Hawks wouldn't stand for back-to-back losses at the United Center. Brent Seabrook's goal in the seventh minute of the second period began the comeback, and Patrick Sharp tied it 2-2 with a shorthanded goal early in the third. Kris Versteeg and Patrick Kane added points late to post a 4-2 win.

[TOP] Kris Versteeg scored the game-winning goal with 90 seconds left in the game, allowing the Hawks to steal a come-from-behind victory.
[ABOVE] Fans at the Madhouse on Madison respond to a Blackhawks goal.
[OPPOSITE] Patrick Kane steps onto the ice to seek revenge for a 5-1 loss to the Canucks in Game 1.

Western Conference Semifinals

GAME THREE
MAY 5, 2010

The Blackhawks opened Game 3 with a 2-0 lead in the first period — and they never looked back from there. Dustin Byfuglien had his first three goals of the playoffs for the Hawks. His second midway through the second period proved to be the game-winner, and Marian Hossa scored in the third. Antti Niemi made 31 saves, 16 in the first period alone. The Blackhawks took a 5-2 victory at GM Place for a 2-1 lead in the series.

[TOP] Dustin Byfuglien strikes his iconic pose after scoring one of his three goals during Game 3.
[ABOVE LEFT] Captain Jonathan Toews hands off the championship belt, awarded by the players, to Game 3 MVP Dustin Byfuglien.
[ABOVE RIGHT] Joel Quenneville coached the Hawks to a 5-2 victory on hostile ice at GM Place in Vancouver.
[OPPOSITE] Patrick Kane tapes his stick in the locker room prior to Game 3.

GAME FOUR

MAY 7, 2010

With Jonathan Toews' guidance, the Blackhawks moved to within one win of the Western Conference Final. The 22-year-old captain proved his leadership skills on the ice with three goals and two assists against the Canucks. But it was Brent Seabrook who set the tone, scoring just 18 seconds into the first period. The Blackhawks netted four goals on the power play to beat Vancouver 7-4.

[TOP] Tomas Kopecky reacts after scoring during the third period.
[ABOVE] Brent Seabrook congratulates Hawks goalkeeper Antti Niemi (left), who made 26 saves for his third straight win.
[OPPOSITE TOP] Blackhawks fans who made the trek to Vancouver high-five each other prior to Game 4.
[OPPOSITE BOTTOM] Jonathan Toews' five-point night gave him a playoff-leading 18 points. He would finish with 29 points in 22 postseason games.

Western Conference Semifinals

GAME FIVE
MAY 9, 2010

With a 4-1 loss at the United Center, the Hawks missed an opportunity to eliminate the Canucks and move straight to the Western Conference Final. Vancouver took the lead early with a goal from Christian Ehrhoff just 59 seconds into the first period, and Kevin Bieksa followed up with two. Plagued by minor penalty calls, the Hawks were only able to score once, when Jonathan Toews redirected Duncan Keith's shot into the net with 7:09 left.

[TOP] Adam Burish and Jonathan Toews combined efforts to net the Hawks' first — and only — goal of Game 5.
[ABOVE LEFT] Netminder Antti Niemi makes a save on Vancouver's Ryan Kesler.
[ABOVE RIGHT] A fan shows her love for Dustin "Big Buff" Byfuglien and Jonathan "Tazer" Toews.
[OPPOSITE] Niemi made 20 saves in the Blackhawks' 4–1 home loss, sending the action back to Vancouver.

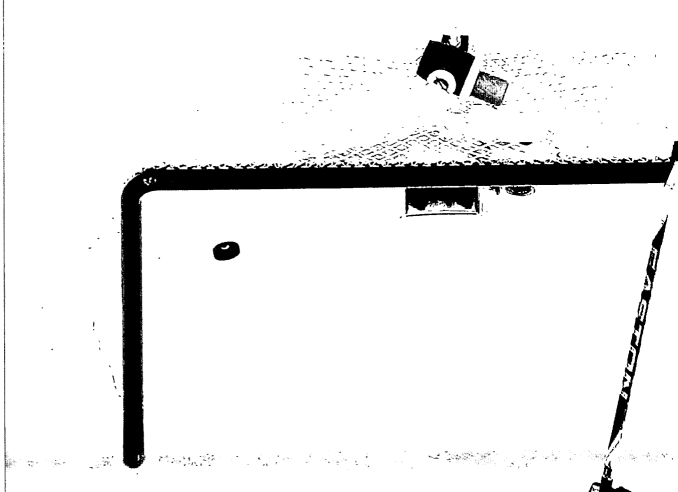

GAME SIX

MAY 11, 2010

Despite valiant efforts from Canucks goaltender Roberto Luongo, there was no stopping the Hawks from taking a Game 6 victory. After being held off in the first period, Troy Brouwer and Kris Versteeg netted two goals within 36 seconds of each other in the second. Vancouver got on the board in the third, but the Hawks scored twice more for a 5-1 rout that gave them a six-game series win over the Canucks and put them in contention for the Western Conference championship.

[TOP] Patrick Kane and goalie Roberto Luongo congratulate each other at center ice after the Hawks' 5–1 win.
[ABOVE] Despite his acrobatics, Luongo couldn't deny Troy Brouwer's second period score.
[OPPOSITE] Dave Bolland scores a shorthanded goal on Luongo at 19:15 of the second period.

TEAM BONDING: THE COMFORT ZONE

BY ANNE E. STEIN

During the playoffs the team set up a players lounge at every road hotel and stocked it with drinks, snacks and flat screen TVs. "The lounge is a big sanctuary for them to relax in," says Senior Director, Team Services Tony Ommen, who notes the team started the lounge tradition during the 2008-09 playoffs. Next door was a private dining area, and each night the lounge was packed with players.

"We're fortunate as a staff knowing that the players get along so well," says head coach Joel Quenneville. "They like each other and like hanging out and trying to make each other better on the ice. They enjoy that quality time being around each other at dinner, at the hotel or playing a hockey game. Guys are comfortable with each other, and they care for one another."

Chicago established a franchise record 23 road wins and during the playoffs won seven straight away from home — nearly breaking the NHL record — starting with Nashville (two wins), Vancouver (three) and San Jose (two).

The key, says alternate captain Patrick Sharp, is pretty simple. "When you're on the road, you spend more time as a team. That's where we want to be. That's where we're in our comfort zone."

When the team had five days between the end of the Vancouver series and the start of Round 3 with San Jose, Coach Q knew they needed a day away from the rink to think about something other than playoff hockey.

The team decided on a trip to Alcatraz Island, which turned out to be many of the players' favorite bonding experience of the season. With half the team dressed in matching black Alcatraz sweatshirts — they didn't anticipate the prison's icy chill — and geared up with headphones for a guided tour, the boys mingled with other tourists and took in the sights.

"A lot of hard work goes into bonding and being a team on the ice, but you still have to have fun," says captain Toews, who like everyone else, relished a day away from the rink.

Winning the Stanley Cup remains the ultimate bonding experience however. "The postgame celebration in the locker room with the guys popping champagne, enjoying the moment, Coach Q soaked in his suit — that was the best, right there," says Toews.

"Parading with your pals in front of two million people is pretty special as well," says forward Bryan Bickell. "To experience that with everybody that was on the team — that's going to be something I remember the rest of my life."

[TOP] Brian Campbell takes in the sights on a ferry ride from San Francisco to Alcatraz Island.
[ABOVE] Troy Brouwer (left) and Jordan Hendry read up on Alcatraz Island during a team outing.
[OPPOSITE] Colin Fraser (left) interviews Brouwer for a Blackhawks TV segment.

[TOP] Brian Campbell (left), Troy Brouwer (center) and Jonathan Toews compete in a game of Mario Kart in the players lounge at the team hotel in San Jose.
[ABOVE] From left to right: Patrick Sharp, Colin Fraser and Brent Seabrook chat over morning coffee while waiting outside the team hotel to head to practice.

VIEW FROM THE BOOTH

WITH PAT FOLEY: TEAM BONDING

I think in hockey a feeling of togetherness and "all for one, one for all" is probably as important, if not more important, than in any other sport. Hockey is a contact sport, and when you know the guy next to you has your back, that makes you bigger, stronger and faster.

When you have a tight team, that team is going to do better than one that is not as cohesive but has more ability. I've seen it dozens of times. Many of our teams in the 1980s had a caring for one another that was really, really strong. In many of those years, the Blackhawks overachieved. Nobody ever picked them to win the division; nobody ever picked them to win a playoff round or to beat the Minnesota North Stars or the St. Louis Blues, but they beat them every year because they were tight.

They would fly into the city the day before, and basically the rule was five minutes — you check into the hotel, throw your bag into the room and meet everyone in the lobby. Everybody on the team went somewhere. That was the point: Everybody went. Some guys would go for 20 minutes and leave for dinner over here or to go with buddies over there, but they always started together, and most of them ended together.

It was a really neat dynamic that they had, and I think now, particularly with the money involved and, to some degree, with the different cultures involved — hockey being a world game — it's harder than ever to do that. But it was striking to me how tight this year's group was, and obviously it served them well. It was very evident watching them play. I think everybody did feel bigger, strong and faster because they knew that the guy next to him had his back. This group was really, really special.

A lot of that comes from individual character. You have to be somebody who's willing to say, "The team is more important than me." We all know what pro sports are like today — it's about me, not we. It's about my highlight on SportsCenter or how I showboat after scoring when the camera is on me. I didn't get the sense that there was very much of that at all with this group.

I think youth was a factor and the leadership — Jonathan Toews is an extremely special individual. For a real young guy given the "C," the way he handled himself was exemplary.

Was there a tighter group in professional sports than the 2009-10 Blackhawks? I doubt it. I think it speaks to the character of the individuals, and when you get a good group of people to come together, you have what we have: champions.

— Pat Foley is the television play-by-by announcer for the Chicago Blackhawks

Western Conference Final

GAME ONE

MAY 16, 2010

San Jose eked out home ice advantage for this best-of-seven series on the last day of the regular season. But the Blackhawks played another exceptional road game after waiting four full days in Shark territory following a 4-2 series win over the Vancouver Canucks. San Jose was first to tally, but Patrick Sharp tied it up 1-1 in the second, and Dustin Byfuglien netted the winning goal with 6:45 left in the third on a slap shot from between the circles.

VIEW FROM THE BOOTH
WITH PAT FOLEY: TEAM BONDING

I think in hockey a feeling of togetherness and "all for one, one for all" is probably as important, if not more important, than in any other sport. Hockey is a contact sport, and when you know the guy next to you has your back, that makes you bigger, stronger and faster.

When you have a tight team, that team is going to do better than one that is not as cohesive but has more ability. I've seen it dozens of times. Many of our teams in the 1980s had a caring for one another that was really, really strong. In many of those years, the Blackhawks overachieved. Nobody ever picked them to win the division; nobody ever picked them to win a playoff round or to beat the Minnesota North Stars or the St. Louis Blues, but they beat them every year because they were tight.

They would fly into the city the day before, and basically the rule was five minutes — you check into the hotel, throw your bag into the room and meet everyone in the lobby. Everybody on the team went somewhere. That was the point: Everybody went. Some guys would go for 20 minutes and leave for dinner over here or to go with buddies over there, but they always started together, and most of them ended together.

It was a really neat dynamic that they had, and I think now, particularly with the money involved and, to some degree, with the different cultures involved — hockey being a world game — it's harder than ever to do that. But it was striking to me how tight this year's group was, and obviously it served them well. It was very evident watching them play. I think everybody did feel bigger, strong and faster because they knew that the guy next to him had his back. This group was really, really special.

A lot of that comes from individual character. You have to be somebody who's willing to say, "The team is more important than me." We all know what pro sports are like today — it's about me, not we. It's about my highlight on SportsCenter or how I showboat after scoring when the camera is on me. I didn't get the sense that there was very much of that at all with this group.

I think youth was a factor and the leadership — Jonathan Toews is an extremely special individual. For a real young guy given the "C," the way he handled himself was exemplary.

Was there a tighter group in professional sports than the 2009-10 Blackhawks? I doubt it. I think it speaks to the character of the individuals, and when you get a good group of people to come together, you have what we have: champions.

— *Pat Foley is the television play-by-by announcer for the Chicago Blackhawks*

Western Conference Final

At high noon for a national TV audience, the Blackhawks took to the ice at the Shark Tank, one of the least accommodating rinks for visiting NHL teams, and played an exceptional road game to win the opener of their much-anticipated showdown against the San Jose Sharks, 2-1. Jason Demers scored on a first period power play for the Sharks, who eeked out home ice advantage for this best-of-seven series on the final day of the regular season by finishing with 113 points, one more than the Blackhawks. But the visitors negated that edge with 60 minutes of energetic play and the superlative goalkeeping of Antti Niemi, who was rapidly converting skeptics portraying him as the supposed "weak link" on the Blackhawks.

After dispatching the Canucks, the Blackhawks spent four full days in San Jose, although coach Joel Quenneville designated Friday as pure recreation. The Blackhawks toured Alcatraz Island, followed by a team meal in San Francisco. The rested Blackhawks dealt with five San Jose power plays — Chicago had none — and prevailed on Patrick Sharp's goal to tie the contest in the second period and Dustin Byfuglien's winner with 6:45 remaining in the third. Niemi stopped 44 of 45 shots, including a spectacular save on Ryane Clowe that had to be seen to be believed. "One of the best, for sure," allowed the goalie when asked to rank his effort.

The Blackhawks, on a road roll, tied a league record with their seventh straight playoff victory on foreign ice by beating the Sharks, 4-2, in Game 2. The Sharks started quickly again, outshooting the Blackhawks 10-3 in the first period, but Niemi faced only 15 thereafter while Andrew Ladd beat Evgeni Nabokov to make it 1-0. Jonathan Toews tied a franchise record by notching at least one point in 11 consecutive playoff games with an assist on Byfuglien's goal, then scored on a power play to boost the Blackhawks' margin to 3-0.

When the Blackhawks finally returned home for Game 3, they stayed in a downtown hotel to mimic their road routine. Coach Q's maneuver succeeded, but it wasn't mints on the pillows that did it. Byfuglien converted on Dave Bolland's feed 12:24 into sudden death to provide a 3-2 triumph before 22,311 in the United Center. The Sharks outshot Chicago in the third period, 18-6, and tied the match on Patrick Marleau's goal with 4:23 remaining in regulation.

Toews assisted twice to surpass the postseason mark of Stan Mikita, who registered points in 12 consecutive playoff games in 1962. "Jonathan has got it all," remarked Mikita.

The Blackhawks bypassed another trip to the airport on a sultry Sunday by sweeping the Sharks with a come-from-behind 4-2 victory in Game 4, ending a series that most experts predicted would go the limit. The Sharks darted to a 2-0 lead, Ladd was lost with a shoulder injury, and Duncan Keith took a puck in the mouth. Not surprisingly, after bleeding profusely and losing seven teeth, Keith soon reappeared to continue his two-way excellence that was a staple during the playoffs. Brent Seabrook, Dave Bolland, Byfuglien (the winner at 14:05 of the third) and Kris Versteeg scored for the Blackhawks, who advanced to the Stanley Cup Final for the first time since 1992.

Their opponent was not yet identified — Montreal or Philadelphia — but Toews recognized the Clarence Campbell Bowl as it was brought out on a red carpet. "Not the one we want," said the superstitious captain, who treated the hardware as though it were radioactive.

"NOT THE ONE WE WANT," SAID THE SUPERSTITIOUS CAPTAIN, WHO **TREATED THE HARDWARE** AS THOUGH IT WERE RADIOACTIVE.

GAME ONE
MAY 16, 2010

San Jose eked out home ice advantage for this best-of-seven series on the last day of the regular season. But the Blackhawks played another exceptional road game after waiting four full days in Shark territory following a 4-2 series win over the Vancouver Canucks. San Jose was first to tally, but Patrick Sharp tied it up 1-1 in the second, and Dustin Byfuglien netted the winning goal with 6:45 left in the third on a slap shot from between the circles.

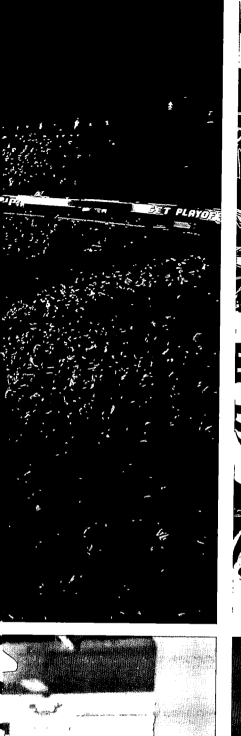

[TOP] Antti Niemi handled San Jose's offensive attack, posting a personal playoff-high 44 saves in the Hawks' 2-1 victory.
[ABOVE] From left to right: Patrick Sharp, Colin Fraser and Brent Seabrook prepare the championship belt for Game 1 MVP "Nemo" Niemi.
[OPPOSITE TOP] Home ice advantage wasn't enough to push the Sharks past the Hawks in front of 17,562 fans at HP Pavilion.
[OPPOSITE BOTTOM] Brian Campbell works on his stick while Equipment Assistant Jim Heintzelman (left) and Equipment Manager Troy Parchman (right) prepare for the morning skate prior to Game 1.

GAME TWO

MAY 18, 2010

The Hawks were already ahead 3-0 midway through the second period when Patrick Marleau beat out Antti Niemi for a power-play goal. Marleau went on to score again, but his efforts didn't stack up to the onslaught of shots faced by Evgeni Nabokov from Andrew Ladd, Dustin Byfuglien, Jonathan Toews and Troy Brouwer. The 4-2 success was the Hawks' seventh straight road win, breaking an 18-year-old club mark and tying a Stanley Cup Playoffs record.

[TOP LEFT] Marian Hossa tapes his stick in solitude prior to the Game 2 matchup.

[TOP RIGHT] A focused coach Joel Quenneville leads his squad from the dressing room into the hostile Shark Tank.

[ABOVE] Dave "The Rat" Bolland pestered the Sharks and made key plays throughout the series.

[OPPOSITE] Patrick Sharp (left) and Troy Brouwer celebrate Brouwer's third period insurance goal that put the Hawks up 4-2.

Western Conference Final

GAME THREE
MAY 21, 2010

Coach Joel Quenneville, quite aware that his boys of winter respond to mints on their pillows, replicated the road ritual by putting them in a local hotel before Game 3 at the United Center. The Blackhawks made it work by beating the Sharks, 3-2, on Dustin Byfuglien's overtime goal off Dave Bolland's feed to ignite a grand Friday night celebration 12:24 into sudden death before 22,311 fans.

[TOP] Hawks legend Stan Mikita (left) congratulates Jonathan Toews on breaking his record for points in consecutive playoff games, after Toews nabbed a point in his 12th straight, a 3-2 victory over San Jose.

[ABOVE] Actor Vince Vaughn (center), with wife Kyla Weber, pounds the glass after a Blackhawks goal.

[OPPOSITE] Brent Seabrook and teammates bow their heads for the national anthem before taking a 3-2 victory on home ice.

GAME FOUR

MAY 23, 2010

On a sultry May Sunday, thousands who suffered through a rough winter ventured into the United Center to watch the Blackhawks sweep the Sharks and advance to the Stanley Cup Final for the first time since 1992. The final score was 4-2, but as was the case throughout the series, nothing came easily, not even for the Western Conference champions.

[TOP] The famous lions outside the Art Institute of Chicago show their Blackhawks pride.
[ABOVE] Duncan Keith lost seven teeth after taking a puck to the mouth in the second period, but he quickly returned to log a team-high 22 minutes of ice time.
[OPPOSITE] The capacity United Center crowd honors the 2010 Western Conference champions.

CHAPTER FOUR
HOCKEY'S BEST TEAM

HOCKEY'S BEST TEAM BY BOB VERDI

On Saturday night of Memorial Day weekend, the Blackhawks won their first game in a Stanley Cup Final since 1973 by outlasting Philadelphia in a wild series opener, 6-5. It was also the first Cup final contest at the United Center, and coach Joel Quenneville aptly characterized the fireworks as a "shootout at O.K. Corral."

Imagine the prevailing wildness had not the top line on either team been blanked. As it was the Blackhawks got two goals from Troy Brouwer, plus scores by Kris Versteeg, Dave Bolland and Patrick Sharp to precipitate a 5-5 situation after 40 minutes that included an early exit by Michael Leighton, the ex-Hawk goalie who had been so instrumental to the Flyers' startling surge from No. 7 Eastern Conference seed through to the finals. Brian Boucher, another former Hawks masked man, yielded the only goal of the third period — by Tomas Kopecky, inserted into the lineup for the ailing Andrew Ladd, at 8:25, on a feed from Versteeg.

Predictably the teams tightened up in Game 2, a white-knuckle 2-1 decision for the Blackhawks. Marian Hossa ended a dry spell in the second period, and Ben Eager scored 28 seconds later, leaving the heavy lifting to Antti Niemi, who was up to the task. He made 15 saves in the second period, 14 in the third and was hailed by United Center fans chanting his name during an on-ice interview after the game. There were 72 hits and 33 blocked shots in 60 taut minutes, plus playoff angst. Kopecky and Daniel Carcillo went nose-to-nose; Philadelphia's Chris Pronger and Eager also chatted at the buzzer.

Having visited General Motors Place and HP Pavilion, the Hawks were prepared for the patois of another enthusiastic fan base in Philadelphia's Wachovia Center. They were not overwhelmed, only outscored, 4-3, when Claude Giroux tallied 5:59 into OT of Game 3. Two video reviews were required earlier: One showed that Simon Gagne did not score on Niemi; another testified that Niklas Hjalmarsson swept a puck away just in time after Scott Hartnell's shot eluded Niemi. Patrick Kane tallied on a breakaway early in the third for a 3-2 Chicago lead, but Ville Leino matched it 20 seconds later. The Flyers rode that momentum to a 5-3 victory in Game 4, building a 4-1 lead before the Blackhawks rally, only to succumb on a Mike Richards empty-netter.

Coach Q juggled his lines for Game 5 at the United Center, and the Blackhawks answered with perhaps their finest first period of the season toward a resounding 7-4 victory. The Toews-Kane-Byfuglien unit was broken up and spread out, but as the captain pointed out, "When you play as a team, it doesn't matter who you're playing with, and tonight we were moving our legs."

Brent Seabrook, Bolland and Versteeg scored during a six-minute burst, much to the delight of Michael Jordan, who showed up just like his statue outside: wearing a No. 19 Toews sweater. Byfuglien gathered two goals, two assists and nine hits, including a robust check on arch-enemy Pronger, who was on the ice for six Chicago goals and serving penalty time for a seventh.

[OPPOSITE] A raucous United Center crowd salutes veterans and the USO of Illinois as Jim Cornelison belts out the national anthem before Game 1 of the Stanley Cup Final.

THE RED LIGHT NEVER DID MAKE AN APPEARANCE, BUT THE BLACKHAWKS GAVE A GREEN LIGHT TO AN ALTERNATIVE FOR GAME 7: A PARADE IN CHICAGO FOR THE BEST TEAM IN HOCKEY.

Kane skated behind the Flyers' cage, manned by Leighton, from left to right. Suddenly, the Blackhawks' sprightly young forward started to shake, rattle and roll. He tossed his stick in the air, then his gloves, all the better to raise his fists in the air, as if he had just matched all the numbers on a lottery ticket.

There was a moment or two of awkward silence in the normally raucous Wachovia Center. Then, in fire drill formation, the Hawks emptied from the visitors bench. Kane knew it first, though the red light failed to ignite. After 49 years and 4:06 of overtime in Game 6, the Blackhawks had won the Stanley Cup. Kane's shot from the left circle slipped through Leighton but then hid somewhere in the tangled web of the net. "I saw it … it was in," exclaimed Kane. "It was over."

The Stanley Cup was in the Wachovia Center on this summery Wednesday night, but so were the Flyers and their fans, a sea of orange. The Flyers had been in dire circumstances before, down 3-0 in a series to Boston and 3-0 to the Bruins in Game 7. So the Hawks were well aware that the 16th victory in their playoff marathon would be exacting, and it was all of that.

The Flyers, trailing 3-2, tied the game on a goal by Hartnell with only 3:59 remaining in the third period. Niemi had to stone Jeff Carter a couple minutes later to preserve the deadlock. Sudden death is just that, and so in a way is Game 7, and the Blackhawks did not want to tempt fate by playing it on June 11, exactly two months since their regular season concluded and that magic number — 16 — appeared on the locker room message board.

So Kane scored for the historic 4-3 conquest, and he could have danced all night. The Blackhawks spilled onto the ice and stayed there, for pictures, interviews and serial hoistings of the Stanley Cup, from Conn Smythe Trophy winner Toews to Hossa to everyone who made it happen — players, coaches, trainers and the men in suits who uttered "One Goal" in their sleep. Rocky Wirtz, John McDonough, Jay Blunk, Stan Bowman, Kevin Cheveldayoff, Al MacIsaac, Scotty Bowman and on and on into the morning. The red light never did make an appearance, but the Blackhawks gave a green light to an alternative for Game 7 on June 11: a parade in Chicago for the best team in hockey. ∎

[OPPOSITE] Chicago Bulls legend Michael Jordan showed his support for the Blackhawks inside the United Center at Game 5 and outside, as his statue was decked out in a Jonathan Toews sweater and helmet.

GAME ONE

MAY 29, 2010

In a wild opener of the Stanley Cup Final, the Blackhawks outlasted the Flyers, 6-5, at the United Center. The victory was the first in the final for the Hawks since 1973 and their first final exam since moving from Chicago Stadium. Troy Brouwer and Patrick Sharp each scored, and Tomas Kopecky tallied the winner at 8:25 of the third period — the only goal in the last 20 minutes after a frenetic 40 that had fans on their feet.

[TOP] The Blackhawks revived the infamous "Blues Brothers" car and used it to stir up fan support throughout the city during the playoffs.

[ABOVE LEFT] A young fan shows off his playoff "beard."

[ABOVE RIGHT] Kris Versteeg scored the eighth goal in the wild 6–5 Hawks victory.

[OPPOSITE] Veteran Flyers defenseman Chris Pronger would prove to be a formidable adversary for John Madden and the Blackhawks throughout the series.

GAME TWO

MAY 31, 2010

Game 2 was a lot easier on the coaching staffs, if not the 22,275 fans in the United Center who hung around after the Blackhawks' white-knuckle 2-1 victory to salute the unquestioned star of the evening, Antti Niemi. Marian Hossa and ex-Flyer Ben Eager scored 28 seconds apart in the second period; then it was up to Niemi to make it happen, and he was up to the task as the Flyers showered him with 15 shots in the third period.

[TOP] Dustin Byfuglien (center) battles for position with Scott Hartnell and Matt Carle in front of the Flyers net.

[ABOVE] Tomas Kopecky (right) and Flyer Daniel Carcillo got matching minors for roughing and unsportsmanlike conduct respectively with 2:33 to play.

[OPPOSITE] Duncan Keith (left) and Antti Niemi hug it out on the ice after the Hawks 2–0 win, which was in large part thanks to Niemi's 33 saves.

GAME THREE
JUNE 2, 2010

Philadelphia snapped the Blackhawks' seven consecutive road game-winning streak with a 4-3 nailbiter at the Wachovia Center. The Flyers got on the board first but coughed up two leads on tallies by defensemen Duncan Keith and Brent Sopel. Patrick Kane scored the go-ahead goal early in the third period with the Flyers tying it up 3-3 just 20 seconds later. Claude Giroux put home a deflection 5:59 into OT.

[TOP] Replay showed Niklas Hjalmarsson narrowly prevented a Philadelphia goal.
[ABOVE LEFT] Brent Seabrook gets physical with the Flyers.
[ABOVE RIGHT] Dave Bolland walks the runway to the Blackhawks charter plane heading to Philly for Game 3.
[OPPOSITE] Ben Eager (left) fist-bumps teammates as they exit the locker room for pregame warm-ups.

GAME FOUR

JUNE 4, 2010

Antti Niemi was slammed in the first period, starting with a power-play goal by Mike Richards just 4:35 into the contest. Patrick Sharp's long-range slapper from the point brought the Hawks back into the game, but the Flyers made it 3-1 before hitting the locker room. After a silent second, the third period opened with a Flyers goal that deflected off the back of Kris Versteeg. Goals from Dave Bolland and Brian Campbell weren't enough to top Philadelphia.

[ABOVE] Brent Sopel fights for the puck with Philadelphia's Darroll Powe during Game 4.

[OPPOSITE TOP] Patrick Kane listens to music to get himself pumped up as he enters the arena.

[OPPOSITE BOTTOM] Marian Hossa signs autographs for fans who have gathered outside the team hotel in Philadelphia.

GAME FIVE

JUNE 6, 2010

After two defeats in Philly, the Blackhawks returned home for Game 5 with an anxious attitude and juggled lines. The result was a 7-4 rout of the Flyers and a 3-2 series lead. Coach Joel Quenneville broke up his top trio of Toews-Kane-Byfuglien. But more importantly, the Blackhawks noted how they were moving their legs as a unit, particularly during a brilliant first period, quite possibly their best of the season.

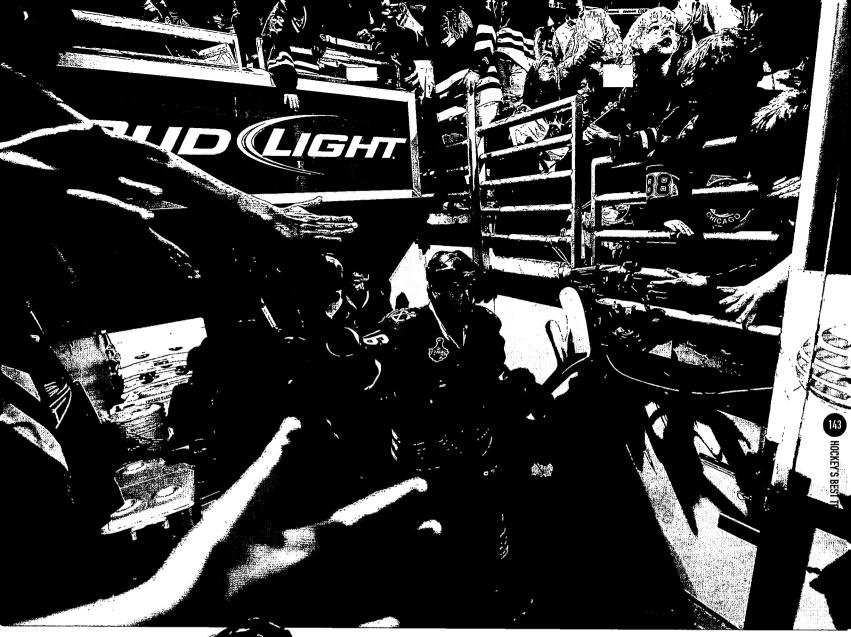

[TOP] Young fans greet Dave Bolland as he heads from the locker room to the ice.
[ABOVE LEFT] From left to right: Brian Campbell, Patrick Kane and Patrick Sharp rejoice after Kane's 2nd period score.
[ABOVE RIGHT] NBA legend and Hall of Famer Michael Jordan donned a Toews sweater to take in Game 5 at the United Center.
[OPPOSITE] Chicago's WGN Radio 720 supported the Blackhawks by displaying a Jonathan Toews banner during the Stanley Cup Final.

GAME SIX

JUNE 9, 2010

When it has been 49 years since your last Stanley Cup, do you really need a red light to make it official? Absolutely not. On a Wednesday night in the Wachovia Center, Chicago's boys of winter captured Game 6, 4-3 in overtime, and the Blackhawks were NHL champions for the first time since 1961. Fans will long remember the image of Patrick Kane dropping his stick and gloves after beating Michael Leighton from the bottom of the left circle 4:06 into OT.

[TOP] Assistant coach John Torchetti (left), head coach Joel Quenneville (center) and assistant coach Mike Haviland react after realizing Patrick Kane's shot went in.
[ABOVE] Chairman Rocky Wirtz (left), Executive Vice President Jay Blunk (center) and President John McDonough enjoy the moment in the elevator as they head down to the ice to accept the Stanley Cup.
[OPPOSITE TOP] Kane is the first to recognize that the Blackhawks have won the Stanley Cup.
[OPPOSITE BOTTOM] After initial confusion on whether the puck actually went in, the Hawks bench rushes the ice to celebrate Kane's game-winning goal.

DEFINING MOMENT

BY BLACKHAWKS FRONT OFFICE MEMBERS

O n the brink of a Stanley Cup title for the first time in 49 years, much of the Blackhawks front office made the trip to Philadelphia for what was to be an epic Game 6 victory while some stayed back in Chicago, hoping to celebrate with hockey's greatest fans.

STAN BOWMAN: GENERAL MANAGER

We were crowded into a small room in the press box. It was myself, Chevy (Kevin Cheveldayoff), Marc Bergevin, Mark Kelley and Steph Waite. We all stood up and just looked at each other because nothing was happening except Kane was skating down the ice. I remember pointing to the net and saying, "I think that puck went in"; the goalie wasn't reacting like he had it. But we waited and waited and waited, and then we all just hugged each other and made the mad dash to get down to the ice. From that point on it was just euphoria.

ADAM KEMPENAAR: DIRECTOR, NEW MEDIA AND PUBLICATIONS

I didn't realize how superstitious I was until Game 6. When the Flyers scored two in a row to take a 2-1 lead in the middle frame, I bolted out of the press box for the media room downstairs to try to swing the momentum. I found the exact same chair I'd sat in and exact same TV I'd watched during the third period of Game 4 when the Blackhawks reduced a three-goal deficit to one and almost stole the game. Just a few minutes after taking my lucky seat, Patrick Sharp evened the score. Then Andrew Ladd gave the Hawks a 3-2 lead at 17:43. It was working!

With about five minutes to play — the Blackhawks clinging to that one-goal lead — two Wachovia Center employees decided to stand right next to me and root for the Flyers. Sure enough, Scott Hartnell tied it up to force overtime. I vowed that if they were still standing there at the start of OT, I'd retreat to another spot rather than let them ruin whatever mystical boost I believed I was giving the Blackhawks. They left during the intermission, but as soon as the puck dropped, they returned and resumed cheering. I couldn't take it. I started roaming the basement, looking for another location to enjoy the action, and found my way into the empty post-game interview room. The TV didn't have any sound, but it was only about a minute later that Patrick Kane's actions would say it all. When he flung his gloves off and sped down the ice to celebrate, I just remember turning and running down the hallway as fast I could, heart pounding, in search of a friendly face to confirm that it was true. At one point I slipped and almost took a nosedive into the cement. It would have been worth it. The Blackhawks were the Stanley Cup champs!

ANNIE CAMINS: DIRECTOR, YOUTH HOCKEY

I was at the Blackhawks road watch party at Joe's Bar on Weed Street with a bunch of fans and basically all of the staff who didn't travel to Philly. There had to be about 500 of us. We pulled out the champagne during overtime. We were just waiting for it. It was pretty presumptuous, I guess. I was with two of my friends about five feet from the TV; we were just kind of holding hands. I saw the goal go in though, so I jumped up and yelled, "They scored! They scored!" We were all cheering in the bar; nobody really knew there was any question about it. We saw Kane celebrating and knew it went in. We kind of glanced back at the TV, but nobody really cared at that point. We were crazy celebrating. The music and cheering were so loud, and champagne was spraying everywhere.

TONY OMMEN: SENIOR DIRECTOR, TEAM SERVICES

I was in the coaches office watching the TV feed with a couple coaches and staff members. When Kane scored we were all kind of excited but also stunned because we weren't 100 percent sure it went it. We all raced to the bench immediately, but we couldn't get to it because of the security. Brad Aldrich (video coach) turned around and ran back into the locker room; he saw the replay, and then ran right back out. We fought our way to the bench, and he was yelling at Joel, "It's in! It's in!" And that's when they all went nuts. We all just jumped on the bench, and by that time Kaner was down on top of Niemi, and everyone was piling on him. It was pure shock more than anything, just amazement that we accomplished that. You work hard every day to build up to that moment, and then for it to happen, it almost was surreal. It didn't quite feel like it was actually happening.

MATT DOMINICK: PRODUCER, NEW MEDIA

With about 10 minutes left in the third period, every photographer and video guy was packed in the Zamboni entrance, ready to go out onto the ice if the series ended. They brought out the Stanley Cup and set it on top of the case. It seemed like the second they put it down, Philly tied it up, and the Cup was put back in and wheeled away. We were all stuck in the tunnel during the break, which was awful.

When Kane scored, I had no idea what was going on because there was a little bit of a delay. There wasn't a reaction from Philly, and nobody was really cheering, so I thought the game was still going on. Commissioner Bettman was standing right next to me, watching the same TV screen. They showed the replay, and it was definitely a goal. Everyone just started yelling, "Go! Get out on the ice!"

MARIE SUTERA: DIRECTOR, HUMAN RESOURCES

The team chartered in the players' families, and we rented out three or four suites. When we won the families were a little confused, just like everyone else. We watched the replay and some of the kids really picked up on it first, "Oh my God, we won." Then it was just complete commotion. We had an escort to get us down to the ice level. Standing in line with the families, they just couldn't wait to get out there.

The plane trip back to Chicago was crazy too. Most of the families passed out from complete exhaustion, but I was wide awake. When we landed the pilot said, "I've just heard that the plane with the players is about five minutes behind us. Do you want to wait to let them get off first?" We all said yes, and our plane taxied to the side. Then the players landed. I remember Brent Sopel tracking down our plane and waiting for his wife and kids to come down. It was really sweet.

JAY BLUNK: EXECUTIVE VICE PRESIDENT

The transition from the locker room to the team bus and the charter was seamless. With each passing minute the feeling of disbelief began to dissolve into reality. The Blackhawks had won the Stanley Cup. As we boarded the aircraft, I could see the glint of the Cup toward the back, confirming that I wasn't dreaming. I would steal a glimpse of it throughout the flight, reassuring me this was no fire drill — the Cup was ours. Music, cocktails and lively conversation were in abundance, focusing primarily on the details of the last few minutes of Game 6 which would bond everyone on that plane forever.

Eventually some on the flight dozed, losing the battle with the fatigue that comes with the highs and lows of a championship series. I chose to savor every second, knowing the rarity of the event. I secretly hoped we would never land, that we might carry on the celebration forever. But as the landing gear rumbled into position, I took one more look out the window at the Chicago skyline, the sun perilously close to turning the evening into morning. The plane came to a stop, and Joel barked an order for "Jonny" to carry the Cup off first. The players marched off behind their captain, disappearing into a sea of flashing blue and red lights from an army of emergency vehicles stationed to greet us. I catalogued as many memories as I could, hoping to recreate for my children that magical experience of flying home with the Stanley Cup.

The Celebration Begins

Humble and hardworking, Blackhawks captain Jonathan Toews is used to winning. Prior to turning pro, Toews had already collected four gold medals in international competition with Team Canada. Then in 2010, he earned an Olympic gold medal in his home country, was named MVP of the playoffs and won the Stanley Cup. But even Toews wasn't 100 percent convinced that the Blackhawks had won the Cup until it was brought onto the ice.

"It happened so fast. You wanted to be everywhere at once and with every single guy," says Toews. "There are only so many things you can do to grasp that moment."

The Stanley Cup victory celebration started with just one guy, Patrick Kane, because he was the only person who was absolutely sure that his goal was safely tucked into the Flyers net.

"We wanted it to be true, but we weren't going to give it a full-hearted celebration until we knew that it was in fact a goal," Toews says. "I remember leaning over because I was tired from the shift, and I was looking at the Jumbotron, and it was really unclear to me whether the puck went in or not.

After a few stunned seconds and a couple of replays later, the reality sunk in and a joyful Kane, who was shedding equipment as he pumped his arms and skated down the ice, was joined by all of his teammates. It took a few more instant replays to convince Blackhawks fans that yes, the championship drought was over. And yes, the celebration could begin.

"It was a weird moment," recalls Toews, who still had doubts until he actually held the Cup. "Then I knew they weren't going to take it away from us, that it was real and actually happening."

After congratulating Blackhawks ownership and management, NHL Commissioner Gary Bettman announced: "Jonathan Toews, come hoist the Stanley Cup."

The Cup, starting with Toews, was lifted, kissed and passed from player to player. Marian Hossa got it second; after the Slovak superstar lost the Cup finals two years in a row, Toews couldn't wait to pass it on to the veteran who bet everything on this young Hawks team. The third guy to get it was former Flyer and alternate captain Patrick Sharp.

Players were quickly joined by moms, dads, wives and kids who were flown to Philadelphia by the organization to enjoy the game. Chicago fans moved down toward the ice to cheer their heroes, and Sharp skated with the Cup in front of the glass to share the victory with them.

The party and the Cup then moved from the ice to the locker room, where coach Joel Quenneville, General Manager Stan Bowman and President John McDonough, dressed in suits, were soaked with champagne.

"That was a special moment," said Toews of the locker room celebration with teammates, coaches, family and front office personnel. "It was absolutely amazing."

— Anne E. Stein

"IT HAPPENED SO FAST. YOU WANTED TO BE EVERYWHERE AT ONCE AND WITH EVERY SINGLE GUY," SAYS TOEWS. "THERE ARE ONLY SO MANY THINGS YOU CAN DO TO GRASP THAT MOMENT."

[TOP] Troy Brouwer shares the Stanley Cup with his wife, Carmen.
[ABOVE] Niklas Hjalmarsson steals a kiss from his girlfriend, Elina.
[OPPOSITE TOP] Blackhawks Chairman Rocky Wirtz (left) hugs Duncan Keith.
[OPPOSITE BOTTOM] An elated Joel Quenneville celebrates his first Stanley Cup as a head coach.

[TOP] Hawks strength and conditioning coach Paul Goodman relishes his moment on the ice with the Stanley Cup.

[ABOVE] Patrick Sharp (left) and Jonathan Toews pose for a quick photo.

[OPPOSITE TOP] Kris Versteeg shares a bottle of champagne with Blackhawks fans after the win.

THEY SAID IT

"I've been with the Blackhawks for 15 years and working in hockey for 26. Winning the Stanley Cup has always been a dream. When you're a kid, that's what you do — imagine yourself winning the Cup. It was amazing to have my wife, Whitney, there to celebrate. There's so much responsibility put on our wives during the season because we're never home. She was crying, and I was just so happy for her. She deserved it as much as I did."

TROY PARCHMAN
EQUIPMENT MANAGER

THEY SAID IT

"For me it was the emotion that had balled up inside of me for 25 years. You hoped it was going to happen, but you couldn't control it. It's something that I'd dreamt about since I was a kid and especially after I turned pro. You can't describe the feeling. Like the commercial said, there's no words to describe it."

MARC BERGEVIN
DIRECTOR OF PLAYER PERSONNEL

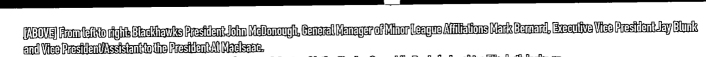

[ABOVE] From left to right: Blackhawks President John McDonough, General Manager of Minor League Affiliations Mark Bernard, Executive Vice President Jay Blunk and Vice President/Assistant to the President Al MacIsaac.
[OPPOSITE TOP] Chairman Rocky Wirtz and his son Danny celebrate with the Stanley Cup while Rocky's daughter Elizabeth looks on.

THEY SAID IT

"Leading up to that day, I had thought about that moment because I was hopeful that we'd win it. What better way to share that moment with my dad than pass the Cup to him? He was obviously a big part of my life, but he was also a big part of our team, helping us earn that Cup with his experience and insight. That exchange really served a dual purpose for me: It was something special for us to win it, and it was my thanks to him for everything he's done for me."

STAN BOWMAN
VICE PRESIDENT/GENERAL MANAGER

[TOP] Kris Versteeg (left) and Colin Fraser (right) congratulate Marian Hossa.
[ABOVE] Brent Sopel takes a photo with his family and the Stanley Cup.

VIEW FROM THE BOOTH

WITH JOHN WIEDEMAN: STANLEY CUP FINAL GAME 6

We were ahead going into the third period when Scott Hartnell scored. First I thought, well, looks like we're going to overtime; and second, Hartnell is killing us. He has two here tonight, and I don't want to see him get a hat trick and force a Game 7.

The home team had won every game up to that point. A Game 7 would have been the worst case scenario, but that was the ray of hope I was hanging on to: If somehow we aren't able to win this thing tonight, at least we'll have Game 7 in front of our fans.

I remember turning to my broadcast partner Troy Murray during the break before overtime and saying, "Philly won't go away, but I really think we can win this tonight. I think we can win it all right here." He said, "I do too, but they're going to have to really dominate in overtime or Philly's going to take control."

When overtime began, Philly had an incredible chance to win it. Duncan Keith got his shinpad on a shot from Mike Richards. I kind of held my breath, and I thought to myself, "God I hope that's not the game winner." Antti Niemi was able to turn it wide in the end, and we dodged a bullet.

Brian Campbell got the puck into the Philly zone to set up the winner. Andrew Ladd did something in the corner because I remember he had just barely gotten the puck around to Campbell. I said from the booth: "Nice play by Campbell to keep it alive at the point. Campbell moves it down to Patrick Kane on the left half boards…"

Kane moved along the goal line toward the net, and I thought to myself, "Man if he shoots from there and wins it, this is right in front of me." Our broadcast position was almost a perfect angle.

But I have to admit that even I was a little confused. Even though I saw Kane celebrating after the shot, I didn't know where the puck was. I didn't see it in the net immediately. I saw some of the Philly players and some of the Blackhawks turning up ice as if the shot had missed the net. For a second there you hear a hesitation in my voice. "He shoots, he scor — oh wait, it looks like Leighton got a piece of it, and it trickled wide."

Michael Leighton moved in the crease, looking one way, then the other, and he kind of slumped a little bit. And then I saw Darroll Powe, his shoulders just dropped and went lifeless. Kane skated around behind the net and out toward center ice with his gloves off, celebrating, and Patrick Sharp joined him. I looked in the back of the net and underneath the padding — and there was the very back of the puck.

Goal.

I had thought about how I was going to call that moment. I remember pausing before walking into the building and thinking, "Is it really going to end tonight? It has been 49 years."

Knowing that it might happen, I had to make sure I blew the roof off that call or I wasn't doing my job. So many great fans have been patient and waiting for the Cup, and now it was finally here. I just had to do the moment justice, even with the confusion of the celebration and no red light. I was so full of adrenaline at that point, and then we saw the replay. I knew what I had to do.

— *John Wiedeman is the radio play-by-play announcer for the Chicago Blackhawks*

PLAY HARD

THEY SAID IT

"Obviously the celebration on the ice and everything that went along with it was overwhelming. This was the first opportunity that Stan (right) and I had to really congratulate each other after all the different things we worked so closely together on throughout the year. It was just a very emotional moment. We achieved the ultimate goal."

KEVIN CHEVELDAYOFF
ASSISTANT GENERAL MANAGER/SENIOR DIRECTOR,
HOCKEY OPERATIONS

[TOP] Blackhawks executives and hockey operations personnel bask in the glow of the Cup.
[OPPOSITE BOTTOM] John Madden breaks out his dance moves in the Blackhawks locker room.

Oh, What a Night!

PHILADELPHIA — At 1:57 Thursday morning, about three hours after the Blackhawks won the Stanley Cup, John Madden hoisted the silver jug above his head and walked it out of a visitors locker room ripe with the aroma of champagne and smoke. The merriment had lasted almost as long as the game, so it was time to head to Chicago where the party would have no expiration date. Besides, the new champions — who had dug so deep since October for whatever it took — had run out of cigars.

One by one, players who had nothing to do with the 49-year itch but embraced with such passion the organization's fiat to scratch it, threaded their way through corridors of the otherwise deserted Wachovia Center, toward the team bus, all eyes on Stanley. There was a seat waiting for this venerable trophy on the charter flight, 10D, right by the card table, and before wheels were up at about 3 a.m., Chicago's boys of winter made sure this most welcome passenger was secure, its seatbelt fastened tightly.

"HOW ABOUT THITH?" exclaimed Duncan Keith, the great, dentally-challenged defenseman. "IS THITH THOMETHING OR WHAT?"

The red light behind Michael Leighton still hasn't ignited. But at 4:06 of overtime in Game 6 of this stirring final series, Patrick Kane knew his shot from the left had slithered through the pads of Philadelphia's goalie. An awkward moment ensued as the fastest sport on earth slipped into neutral, but then No. 88 threw his gloves in the air, and teammates began jumping on each other. The franchise and its fans had waited since 1961, so why fret about a slight delay until that final is posted? Blackhawks 4, Flyers 3. One Goal. Mission accomplished.

On the ice for another whirl before summer, the victors passed the Cup around like the salt shaker at a team meal. Jonathan Toews, 22, a prodigy who won Olympic gold for his country in February, earned the Conn Smythe Trophy as most valuable player throughout the playoffs, but the captain, not-so-serious now, held that Cup high. Marian Hossa grabbed it, then Patrick Sharp, then Brent Sopel, and on it went, a team picture with Stanley in the middle. The Flyers, a classy organization, made sure that hundreds of Blackhawks fans who found secondary ticket market prices agreeable could crowd the lower bowl well beyond closing time. The Blackhawks, so likeable for the way they engage their supporters, saluted those who made the trip and stayed around for the celebration.

The locker room is small, and it became smaller when waves of family and friends entered after the players had left the ice. Team management had chartered a plane to leave O'Hare Wednesday afternoon for fathers, mothers, wives and children, 165 in all. They were taken to Philadelphia's finest steakhouse upon arrival, then to the Wachovia Center, where the Blackhawks secured multiple suites. There is no telling what this magnanimous gesture cost, especially from the man who resurrected the

Blackhawks without ever uttering hoary homilies like the infamous five-year plan.

"Every one of these players and members of our front office staff has a support cast," said Rocky Wirtz. "They belong here. There is no price attached to this. This is priceless."

This is why Chicago, which once was a place where hockey players went to avoid crowds and commotion, is now a destination. In that locker room the Blackhawks, who were praised for their even tempers and level heads when it mattered, shed their sweaters and inhibitions for Stanley Cup Champion 2010 hats and unbridled revelry. They yelled, they sprayed, they sang "Chelsea Dagger," and they hugged like they hadn't seen each other for years and might never see each other again — or at least until Friday's parade.

Wirtz was doused by Dustin Byfuglien, President John McDonough looked like he'd been through a car wash, and Joel Quenneville gushed about how "coaching these guys was like coaching on auto pilot." Coach Q is famously demure on his role in this miracle, but his point was valid. The will and desire of his athletes to excel, if for no other reason than not to disappoint their mates, represents chemistry of the highest order, a dimension that cannot be taught or fractured. As Toews stated when asked where the party would reconvene in Chicago, "I don't know … but wherever we go, we'll go together."

When the NHL really went international, there was all this talk that players from outside North America might regard the Stanley Cup as just another piece of hardware. But on the Blackhawks roster of United Nations, that is folly. Antti

Niemi, the frugal Finn in goal, regaled about how "this is huge at home … huge at home." Hossa was like a kid who finally got what he wanted on his third Christmas morning. Tomas Kopecky acted as though he had never touched the Cup in Detroit, which he had. And Niklas Hjalmarsson was pacing in place. "My town in Sweden has 90 people," he said. "They watched tonight's game at 2 in the morning, then went to milk cows at 5. They are more tired than I am. Wait until I bring this Cup there. They will not be tired."

For the flight home, the Blackhawks sat for takeoff and landing. Otherwise, it was two hours of mingling, aisle-to-aisle, pictures with the Cup and more hugging. The guys were almost wistful that they would not bond at 30,000 feet again anytime soon. Quenneville sat next to Scotty Bowman, who volunteered, "tough to win, a Stanley Cup." Coach Q rolled his eyes at the Hall of Fame genius. "You've won 12!"

About 4 a.m. in Chicago, the plane touched down at O'Hare. Fire trucks showered the charter with water cannons, and Captain Mellow was summoned to the front with Stanley. The door opened as Toews displayed the Cup for cameras, police officers and assorted others who were too happy to sleep on this historic occasion.

The red light still hasn't gone on in the Wachovia Center, but in Chicago the sun was climbing out of bed for another day, and birds were chirping. The Hawks piled into busses for a destination to continue celebrating.

Where they would go was to be kept quiet, but there was no secret how they would go. They would go together. ■

— *Bob Verdi*

[TOP] Coach Q is sprayed with champagne as he hoists the cup in the locker room.

[ABOVE] Ben Eager (left) and Troy Brouwer look on as Andrew Ladd kisses his name on the Stanley Cup. Ladd first won the prize with the Carolina Hurricanes in 2006.

THEY SAID IT

"John (left) and I had as much relief as we did joy on that flight. We both were overjoyed for our fans. They deserved to celebrate each and every moment with us after the 49-year drought."

JAY BLUNK
EXECUTIVE VICE PRESIDENT

[TOP] Dustin Byfuglien grabs a Blackhawks TV camera to help document the plane ride back to Chicago.
[ABOVE] Bryan Bickell (left) and Duncan Keith show off their battle wounds.
[OPPOSITE TOP] Tomas Kopecky (left) and Marian Hossa kiss the Cup on the plane.

[TOP] The Chicago Fire Department sprayed the plane with water as it taxied into the terminal.

[ABOVE] Captain Jonathan Toews is the first person off the plane with the Stanley Cup.

[OPPOSITE TOP] Andrew Ladd poses with the Cup and firemen from the Chicago Fire Department.

[OPPOSITE BOTTOM] Brian Campbell greets media assembled inside the terminal.

2010 STANLEY CUP PLAYOFFS

PLAYER	POS	GP	G	A	P	+/-	PIM	PP	SH	GW	S	S%	TOI/G
Jonathan Toews	C	22	7	22	29	-1	4	5	0	3	58	12.1	20:58
Patrick Kane	R	22	10	18	28	-2	6	1	1	1	64	15.6	18:54
Patrick Sharp	L/C	22	11	11	22	10	16	3	1	1	76	14.5	17:51
Duncan Keith	D	22	2	15	17	2	10	0	0	0	61	3.3	28:11
Dustin Byfuglien	R	22	11	5	16	-4	20	5	0	5	45	24.4	16:15
Dave Bolland	C	22	8	8	16	6	30	2	2	1	35	22.9	18:39
Marian Hossa	R	22	3	12	15	7	25	0	0	1	73	4.1	18:25
Kris Versteeg	R	22	6	8	14	4	14	0	0	2	55	10.9	17:12
Brent Seabrook	D	22	4	7	11	8	14	1	0	0	39	10.3	24:10
Troy Brouwer	L	19	4	4	8	-1	8	0	0	0	21	19.0	11:01
Niklas Hjalmarsson	D	22	1	7	8	9	6	0	0	0	17	5.9	21:00
Tomas Kopecky	L	17	4	2	6	2	8	1	0	1	28	14.3	13:34
Andrew Ladd	L	19	3	3	6	4	12	0	0	0	23	13.0	12:47
Brent Sopel	D	22	1	5	6	7	8	0	0	0	16	6.3	18:29
Brian Campbell	D	19	1	4	5	11	2	0	0	0	23	4.3	19:34
Ben Eager	L	18	1	2	3	2	20	0	0	1	13	7.7	6:02
John Madden	C	22	1	1	2	-2	2	0	0	0	24	4.2	11:34
Bryan Bickell	L	4	0	1	1	3	2	0	0	0	3	0.0	13:14
Adam Burish	R	15	0	0	0	-1	2	0	0	0	15	0.0	5:34
Jordan Hendry	D	15	0	0	0	-4	2	0	0	0	8	0.0	8:08
Nick Boynton	D	3	0	0	0	2	2	0	0	0	2	0.0	8:22
Colin Fraser	C	3	0	0	0	0	0	0	0	0	1	0.0	8:23

GOALTENDER	GP	MINS	AVG	W	L	OT	EN	SO	GA	SA	SV%	G	A	PIM
Antti Niemi	22	1,321:51	2.63	16	6	-	4	2	58	645	.910	0	0	2
Cristobal Huet	1	20:00	0.00	0	0	-	-	0	0	3	1.000	0	0	0

[OPPOSITE TOP] Word of the Hawks' private after party spread, and hundreds of fans awaited the team's arrival at Harry Caray's in Rosemont around 5 a.m.
[OPPOSITE BOTTOM LEFT] Duncan Keith transports the Cup from the team bus into the restaurant.
[OPPOSITE BOTTOM RIGHT] Jonathan Toews puts Vice President/General Manager Stan Bowman's son, Camden, in the Stanley Cup.

CHAPTER FIVE
SUMMER OF STANLEY

SUMMER OF STANLEY BY BOB VERDI

I am not an expert at estimating crowds, but I would peg the number attending the Blackhawks Stanley Cup victory parade as slightly above 18,000. As many may recall, 18,000 used to be a popular figure around here. That was a familiar refrain for people who didn't like hockey or didn't get it: Even though the old Chicago Stadium often had no empty seats on game nights, there still are no more than 18,000 hockey fans in Chicago.

Well, during the parade, it appeared that there were 18,000 bodies crammed into a multi-layered parking garage at the intersection of Washington and Franklin. Then, as a flotilla of trolleys and double decker busses weaved through the Loop and veered north on Michigan Avenue, the screaming room-only throng grew exponentially.

The question is not whether anybody in the city went to work on this historic occasion because police officers were ubiquitous, on wheels, on foot or on horses. But you know it's something special when even Chicago's finest pause to take pictures of the caravan and applaud the National Hockey League champions.

"Never seen anything like this, the way this place has taken to this team," said Bobby Hull. "Even when they were standing six deep at the Stadium in our glory days, there wasn't the buzz there is now. And certainly not in 1961, when we won the Cup the last time. It just wasn't as big.

"Plus, after we clinched in Detroit, we couldn't come back to Chicago. I'm pretty sure we were on a commercial flight because in that era manangement wouldn't spend a dime to watch an earthquake. There was a snowstorm, so we partied there, and by the time we returned to Chicago the edge was off."

There was a snowstorm of confetti as thousands gathered on sidewalks, hung from overpasses and peered from window wells in buildings along a red sea of humanity. If team management worried about losing generations of support during the extended period of indifference toward this franchise, evidence of renewed affection for the Blackhawks and their sport was evident as far as one could see, or hear.

The last love-in accorded to a local team and its title occurred in 2005 when the White Sox were hailed for their World Series conquest. The Sox completed their sweep of the Houston Astros on Oct. 26. The Blackhawks had lost in Nashville the night before and were in Detroit, where they would lose the night after en route to another winter of virtual invisibility and another "bye" in the playoffs.

If you had suggested then that the Blackhawks would be next, you would have been told to go away for a while to get some rest and come back only when you started to make sense again, preferably with a note from your doctor.

But there were the Blackhawks, in uniform again on June 11, the date when Game 7 of the finals was to be contested at the United Center versus the Philadelphia Flyers, if necessary.

"ABOUT A YEAR AND A HALF AGO, THERE WAS A SIGN THAT WAS DRAPED OVER THE UPPER BALCONY AT THE UNITED CENTER, AND IT SAID THAT THE PRIDE WAS BACK. BUT IT'S NEVER BEEN BACK **GREATER THAN IT WAS TODAY.**"

— PRESIDENT JOHN MCDONOUGH

ROCKY WIRTZ JOHN MCDONOUGH JAY BLUNK STAN BOWMAN AL MACISAAC

KEVIN CHEVELDAYOFF JONATHAN TOEWS '19 PATRICK KANE 88 MAYOR DALEY

CHICAGO TROLLEY & DOUBLE DECKER CO.

THE OFFICIAL CROWD ESTIMATE FROM CITY HALL: 2 MILLION. THAT'S NOT A PARADE; THAT'S A CORONATION.

It was not, because the Blackhawks went into overtime to prevail 4-3 on Wednesday night, so they shed their skates and beards — most of them anyway — to be honored and to honor those who had become inexorably hooked on them and the game they play. Foul weather was forecast, but on this day it did not rain on their reign.

On the stage at Michigan and Wacker, barely visible to those who collected for a long-distance sample of the ambiance across the river, emcee Eddie Olczyk introduced dignitaries such as Governor Pat Quinn and Mayor Richard M. Daley, plus the four Hall of Fame ambassadors, Hull, Stan Mikita, Tony Esposito and Denis Savard, along with Pierre Pilote, defensive stalwart on that 1961 roster.

Then came all the men in suits and sweats who labor behind the scenes; Joel Quenneville and assistants John Torchetti and Mike Haviland, who directed piercing glares at officials in Game 6 but were beaming now; broadcasters Pat Foley, John Wiedeman, Troy Murray and Steve Konroyd; and Kevin Magnuson, son of fallen comrade Keith, who would have relished a ceremony such as this.

Rocky Wirtz Superstar, the owner who never missed a beat or wasted a minute, received a thunderous reaction, as did John McDonough and Jay Blunk, front office wizards. Then came the boys of winter. Kris Versteeg offered a rap song, sort of; Patrick Kane pledged to keep his shirt on this summer and thanked cab drivers everywhere; and captain Jonathan Toews carried the Cup

that players have shared with legions at various establishments since it landed in the wee hours following Game 6.

Just another reason why these guys are so revered: They didn't shrink from the pressure of expectations, and they didn't hide when their "One Goal" was achieved. How many professional athletes so openly share their joy without prompting or hubris?

Just like it would have been before Game 7, Jim Cornelison belted out "The Star-Spangled Banner" with Frank Pellico on the organ. But there was no Game 7. Exactly two months after the regular season ended, initiating a marathon saga that required 16 victories in four different and grueling series, the Blackhawks stood there wearing shorts and smiles.

There was a flyover and fireworks, and Chris Pronger was nowhere to be seen because the Stanley Cup had found its way back to Chicago after an extended absence.

Colin Fraser noted how he'd talked recently to pals from other NHL teams who are already working out in preparation for next season. But the Blackhawks can sleep now, if they are so inclined, for they've restored hockey to its rightful place in Chicago, not only because they won but because of how they won. They took their fans along on this grand journey, and there were more than 18,000 of them.

The official crowd estimate from City Hall: 2 million. That's not a parade; that's a coronation.

"WE WORKED HARD AND PAID THE PRICE
FOR EACH OTHER, BUT MOST OF ALL
WE WANTED TO DO IT FOR OURSELVES
AND YOU FANS. **YOU GUYS ARE THE
GREATEST.** THANK YOU VERY MUCH."

— CAPTAIN JONATHAN TOEWS

"WHAT A DAY, WHAT A RIDE. BEST TIME OF MY LIFE RIGHT NOW, HAVING THIS CROWD HERE WITH THE STANLEY CUP... WHO KNOWS A GOOD DENTIST BY THE WAY? **ANYONE GOT A DENTIST?**"

— ALTERNATE CAPTAIN DUNCAN KEITH

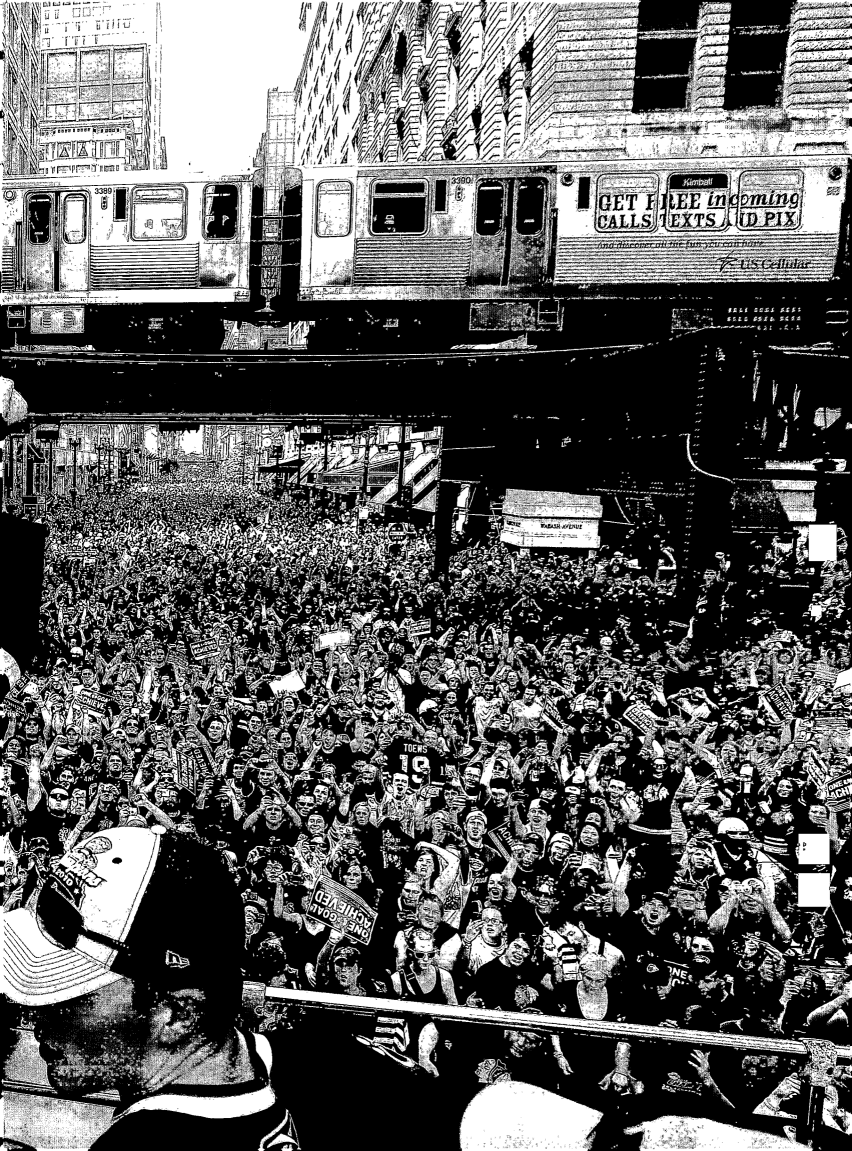

[TOP] Patrick Sharp acknowledges the crowd during the parade rally.
[ABOVE] The view down LaSalle Street as a sea of Chicagoans show their appreciation for the Blackhawks championship.

VIEW FROM THE BOOTH

WITH TROY MURRAY: THE PARADE

I thought I understood what to expect when the Blackhawks won the Stanley Cup. When I won it with Colorado in 1996, we'd had sold-out crowds all season long, so you knew there was good anticipation for the win and the parade.

We had a similar situation in Denver where we had a staging area over by the arena and then took the route through downtown to City Hall. When we came around the corner downtown, I looked and said, "Wow."

There were people packing the streets, and the view was amazing from on top of the fire trucks. They estimated that there were 300,000 people there. Now 300,000 people is a lot of people. I just thought, "This is so cool."

But then came the parade in Chicago.

There was a smattering of people all along the route to get to the start of the parade, from the United Center all the way into downtown. You could see fans out in the streets, waving and cheering. And then you crossed into the downtown area, and when you got around that first corner it was just a sea of red.

It was nothing that I could have expected and way more than what we had in Denver. To see the reception and the excitement and the energy in the crowd was just mind-blowing. Just the magnitude of what that whole day was about was overwhelming — 49 years of expectations coming to a head in downtown Chicago. And the immensity of the city's support, that was the kicker.

It really hit me the first time we crossed a north/south street. We could see the parade route going toward the lake, but what we didn't know was how many people were down the side streets. When you looked down there, you knew some fans couldn't even tell who the people were on the buses. It was amazing that even though they couldn't see Jonathan Toews or Patrick Kane, they were just so eager to be part of that experience, part of the celebration.

The excitement of hockey came back in Chicago at such a feverish pitch and in such a short time. Rocky Wirtz took over and changed the culture of the organization to what he thought was needed for it to become an elite franchise. He brought in President John McDonough, who modernized the team and put the players back in the community. And we wouldn't have gone anywhere without the product on the ice.

It was a progression from two years before when the Hawks had just missed the playoffs, and the fans in Chicago knew there was something special about these young kids. For the expectations to be there in 2009-10 and then to actually celebrate with the Stanley Cup is a testament to the character of the players, coaches and front office.

The Stanley Cup is so special because the organization gets to celebrate with the community that they won it in. And after the parade, for the players to be able to bring the Cup back home, to celebrate with their friends and families, and in hospitals and schools, it's something that you don't see in other sports.

It's a tradition unlike any other, and it's only part of hockey.

— Troy Murray is the radio color analyst for the Chicago Blackhawks

FOLLOWING THE CUP

BY ANNE E. STEIN

From the John Hancock Observatory to the Eiffel Tower and "The Ellen DeGeneres Show" to a Jimmy Buffett concert, the Stanley Cup had an eventful summer. Every member of the 2009-10 Chicago Blackhawks — the players, coaches and executives — had at least one day in their hometowns with the silver chalice.

Parades and parties were the norm, and in nearly every city kids were the focus, with the Cup visiting children's hospitals and local ice arenas. Hometown police and fire departments often got visits too. The Cup took more than a few fishing trips and boat rides — always wearing its own life jacket of course — in lakes throughout Canada.

A variety of food and drink was enjoyed from the Cup's bowl. There was the traditional beer and champagne sipped from the Cup at every stop, but other stuff made its way in there too. Tomas Kopecky enjoyed a traditional Slovakian soup out of the bowl, while Troy Brouwer prepared a feast of Fruit Loops for his wife and sisters-in-law.

The Cup spent plenty of time in Canada but also journeyed to a small town in Sweden with Niklas Hjalmarsson and to Paris, for the first time ever, with goalie Cristobal Huet. It made stops in Finland with Antti Niemi and had several days in Slovakia with Marian Hossa and Kopecky.

No matter where it goes, however, the Cup is accompanied by two "Cup keepers," Hockey Hall of Fame officials who make sure it's safe, superbly shined and thoroughly clean for the next guy, no matter who or what has been in the bowl and no matter how many times the Cup has been kissed, passed or hoisted.

The Cup in Chicago

Immediately after the Blackhawks won the Cup and before it began its journey around the globe, the chalice was squired around Chicago to different bars and clubs, hospitals and baseball games. The Cup was so popular that fans set up a Twitter account just to track where it was sighted.

Coach Joel Quenneville took the Cup to Children's Memorial Hospital and the Stan Mikita Hockey School for the Hearing Impaired. Vice President/General Manager Stan Bowman brought the Cup to his son's school for show-and-tell, and later in the summer the Cup visited the Governor's Mansion, the Illinois State Fair, Northwestern University and Soldier Field.

The Cup Unites North and South

Outside of the Blackhawks victory parade, the Cup's most memorable Chicago appearance came during the annual Cubs-Sox Crosstown Classic in mid-June. It was a true demonstration of the power of the Cup.

White Sox and Cubs fans don't agree on much. But when the Blackhawks, led by captain Jonathan Toews, stepped onto Wrigley Field with the Cup for a pregame appearance, accompanied by their goal song, "Chelsea Dagger," Cubs and Sox players and personnel stood by their dugouts, and fans from both sides roared.

Passing the Cup from one player to the next, the Hawks walked along the ivy-covered outfield walls as the music switched over to Queen's "We Are The Champions." The players then headed back toward the visitors dugout, where Sox

WITH THE CUBS, SOX, BLACKHAWKS AND STANLEY CUP TOGETHER ... IT WAS A SHOW OF SPORTS UNITY NEVER BEFORE SEEN IN CHICAGO.

manager Ozzie Guillen hoisted up Lord Stanley's Cup. Coach Q later brought the Cup over to Cubs manager Lou Piniella, and along with Guillen the three coaches held the Cup together.

The Hawks then made their way to the mound with the Cup, which stood alone on the pitching rubber. Toews plucked a baseball out of the chalice and handed it to Blackhawks President John McDonough. He threw the ceremonial first pitch to hockey fan and Cubs pitcher Ryan Dempster, who lifted the Cup over his head and kissed it.

With Cubs on one side, Blackhawks and the Cup in the middle and Sox on the other, a photo was taken, followed by the Blackhawks' Jim Cornelison singing his famous rendition of the National Anthem. It was a show of sports unity never before seen in Chicago.

Back to "The Tonight Show"

Two days after the Crosstown Classic, Patrick Kane, Toews, Duncan Keith and Brent Seabrook brought the Cup to Burbank, Calif., for a post-victory visit with Jay Leno on "The Tonight Show." The entire team had visited the show during a mid-March road trip to Los Angeles and Anaheim, and Leno had recognized the four Olympic medalists.

After Leno's monologue, Kane led the way to the stage with the Cup, followed by his teammates. Video highlights of the season were

shown, including Kane's Game 6 Cup-winning goal and the shot to the face that knocked out seven of Duncan Keith's teeth.

Duncan presented Leno with a molar — albeit, fake — on a necklace, which he wore throughout the show. The team also gave the host a No. 1 Blackhawks jersey with "Leno" on the back.

The boys were then invited to join The Tonight Show Band for the remainder of the show. After putting the Cup in front of band leader Rickey Minor, the four opened a set with Kane on tambourine, Seabrook on cowbell and Toews and Keith pretending to play guitar. After the show it was off to an Los Angeles nightclub, then back home to Chicago.

Once the Cup returned from California, it began its journey around the world to spend time with each player and coach and their family, friends and fans.

Up in the Air with Patrick Kane

Buffalo, N.Y., native Kane's day with the Cup was a day of highs — literally. First up was a visit to Niagara Falls, specifically the Hurricane Deck at Bridal Veil Falls. Located under the Falls on the American side, the site was marked by a new sign: HurriKane Deck.

Kane had talked about this moment, when he and the Cup would get drenched by the mist from the falls behind him, for months. Friends, family

[OPPOSITE TOP] Three Chicago sports teams come together for a picture before the June 13, 2010, matchup between the Cubs and Sox at Wrigley Field.
[OPPOSITE BOTTOM] With the Stanley Cup resting on home plate, Andrew Ladd and his teammates stand for the national anthem.

and media donned ponchos and took part in the celebration.

For a guy who doesn't like heights, the next few stops were a little scary for the normally fearless Kane. Like a lot of the Blackhawks, he brought the Cup to a local fire department, where he and the Cup and a fireman got on a ladder and were hoisted some 30 feet above the ground — where the ladder proceeded to get stuck, leaving the trio with an extended opportunity to take in an aerial view of Buffalo.

He also visited with iron workers on the fifth story of a construction site. One of the workers, a close family friend of Kane's, had painted "(Buzz) Patrick Kane Wins Stanley Cup" on a fifth floor beam. Buzz was Kane's nickname as a kid.

"Buffalo is my hometown," said Kane. "I still think Chicago is the greatest city in the world, but it's always nice to bring something like this home and bring it back to where you grew up and where your real friends and family are. I think that's important."

Kane and the Cup then stopped at a local rink for photos and autographs with parents and kids, and without the media in tow, the 21-year-old brought the Cup to Roswell Park Cancer Institute. A clearly emotional Kane walked around sharing the Cup with patients and passing out hats and autographs. With his mom and three sisters following — all in tears — Kane made a huge impact on the patients, especially a teenage boy to whom Kane gave his jersey.

The following day Kane and the Cup flew back to Chicago, where the two joined Jimmy Buffett on stage in concert at Toyota Park.

Sharpy's Day in Thunder Bay

For Thunder Bay, Ontario, residents, this was the Cup's second visit in as many years, and third in four years, to their city. Pittsburgh's Jordan Staal brought the Cup to Thunder Bay after the Penguins won the title in 2009. Now it was Patrick Sharp's turn.

[ABOVE] Patrick Kane hoists the Stanley Cup on the newly renamed "HurriKane Deck" at Niagara Falls.
[OPPOSITE TOP] Jimmy Buffett welcomes Kane and the Stanley Cup to the stage during a concert at Toyota Park back in Chicago.
[OPPOSITE BOTTOM] Kane and the Cup visited patients at Roswell Park Cancer Institute in Buffalo, N.Y. Photo courtesy of Roswell Park Cancer Institute.

DAY ONE STARTED WITH A POLICE ESCORT TO CITY HALL AND A VISIT WITH WINNIPEG'S MAYOR, WHO PRESENTED TOEWS WITH **KEYS TO THE CITY.**

Sharp's first stop was the George Jeffrey Children's Centre, serving kids with developmental and physical disabilities. Next up was a visit to the Boys and Girls Club of Thunder Bay, where the kids desperately searched for Sharp's name on the Cup, though it wouldn't be etched on for a few more months.

The kids in Sharp's neighborhood got to see the prize when he brought it to his summer home. Then Sharp, a former baseball player, took it to George Burke Park, a local diamond where he used to play. Two teams instantly stopped playing and mobbed Sharp and the Cup.

Any day with the Cup includes scenic shots, and Sharp took photos with the striking land formation known as the Sleeping Giant in the background. Sharp and the Cup next visited the statue of late runner Terry Fox, a Canadian hero who raised money for cancer research with an across-Canada run.

The night was filled with parties for family and friends, as well as a backstage visit with the band Blues Traveler at the Thunder Bay Blues Festival.

"Any time a parent sees their child achieve their dream and be on top of the world and be happy, it means everything," said Sharp's proud papa, Ian. "That's what being a parent is all about — to see your child work for something and work honest and work hard and to achieve his dream."

Two Days with Toews

There were so many parades, adoring fans and dignitaries scheduled for Toews' celebration that the Blackhawks captain was allotted two days with the Cup in his hometown of Winnipeg.

Day one started with a police escort to City Hall and a visit with the mayor, who presented Toews with keys to the city. He also received moccasins in Chicago Blackhawks colors from the Grand Chief of the First Nations.

After greeting fans on a balcony where a visiting Queen Elizabeth II had stood just a week earlier, Toews, his family and dignitaries had lunch in the mayor's chambers before embarking on a victory parade lined with 10,000 fans. Manitoba's premier announced to Toews and the crowd that a small, remote lake, some 435 miles northwest of Winnipeg, had been renamed Toews Lake.

It wasn't the only honor of the day: Once Toews, his family, the Cup and the Conn Smythe Trophy arrived at the Dakota Community Centre, where Toews grew up playing hockey, it was announced that the arena would be renamed the Jonathan Toews Community Centre.

Winning the Stanley Cup is a dream come true, but to realize how much support, how many fans I have back in Winnipeg and to be able to bring the Stanley Cup back to them, there's nothing that compares, said Toews.

[TOP] A young fan examines Jonathan Toews' gold medal in awe during an event at the Rehabilitation Centre for Children in Winnipeg, Manitoba.
[ABOVE] Patrick Sharp challenged his older brother, Chris, to a game of ping pong. Chris won and got the ultimate prize: the Stanley Cup.

[TOP] Blackhawks President John McDonough brought the Cup to his alma mater, St. Juliana School, in Edison Park, Ill.
[ABOVE] "Cup keeper" Mike Bolt joins a young fan and the Stanley Cup on a ride at the Illinois State Fair in Springfield, Ill. During the Cup's time in the state capital, Chairman Rocky Wirtz and Governor Pat Quinn hosted a party at the Governor's Mansion for local troops. The following day the USO of Illinois hosted a viewing at the Fair where more than 3,000 people got to take a photo with the Cup.

Other visits over the two days with the Cup included the Children's Hospital of Winnipeg, where kids got to see the chalice up close and talk with the playoffs' MVP, and a charity golf outing with 36 teams raising money for the Rehabilitation Centre for Children. Toews went back to "his" community centre on the second day for more photos and autographs, and each day ended with a party.

Hometown Hero

Just three years after taking over the Chicago Blackhawks, President John McDonough had a Stanley Cup to show for his efforts and the efforts of his staff. McDonough's day with the Cup was shared with his wife and children. It began at their home in suburban Chicago, then moved to his mother's gravesite and his childhood home in Chicago's Edison Park neighborhood, where the new owners gave him a tour of the place.

A police escort brought the McDonoughs and the Cup to a local park, where he was greeted by fans, Blackhawks' public address announcer Gene Honda, National Anthem singer Jim Cornelison and local government officials. The party moved to a pub for lunch, then went on to suburban Elk Grove Village, where the McDonoughs have lived for more than two decades.

After a stop at a rehab center and a reception at Elk Grove Village Hall, an estimated 10,000 fans gathered for the Elk Grove Village Hometown Parade to greet McDonough, the mayor and

the Stanley Cup. Another party at a local pub wrapped up the evening for the chalice and the McDonough family.

Motoring with the Cup

Most of the Blackhawks had some kind of hometown parade, and everyone traveled the route in a different way.

Troy Brouwer rode a Zamboni through his hometown of North Delta, British Columbia.

Bryan Bickell and the Cup rode on a vintage fire truck through Orono, Ontario.

Jonathan Toews, the Stanley Cup and the Conn Smythe rode through Winnipeg, Manitoba, in a yellow Corvette convertible.

Brian Campbell rode in a vintage ambulance in the Strathroy, Ontario, Stanley Cup parade.

Duncan Keith, along with the Stanley Cup and the Norris Trophy, rode through Penticton, British Columbia, on a school bus, making stops at a regional hospital and his old rink, the South Okanagan Event Centre, where he was greeted by 5,000 fans.

Jay Blunk, the Blackhawks executive vice president, rode with the Cup in a vintage Volkswagen Bug through his hometown of Danvers, Ill., during the Danvers Days parade.

Dustin Byfuglien strapped the Cup snugly into the front seat of his Maserati and made stops throughout his hometown of Roseau, Minn. Later he and the Cup traveled in a red convertible in the town's first ever Stanley Cup parade. ▨

[ABOVE LEFT] Brent Seabrook hoists the Cup in front of the Strait of Georgia, which sits between Vancouver Island and the mainland coast of British Columbia.
[ABOVE RIGHT] Coach Joel Quenneville (left) poses for a photo with Palace Grill Restaurant owner George Lemperis at his establishment on Madison Street.

[TOP] Troy Brouwer rides a Zamboni during a parade in his hometown of North Delta, British Columbia.
[ABOVE] Fans in Jonathan Toews' hometown of Winnipeg, Manitoba, lined the parade route for a chance to touch the Cup.

Connecting the legacy of hockey and the history of Illinois, the Stanley Cup spent a busy day in the heart of the Land of Lincoln. The trip to Springfield included visits to: the state capitol building (1, 3, 4) where Blackhawks Chairman Rocky Wirtz held a public viewing (2); Abraham Lincoln's bedroom at the Governor's Mansion (6); and the Lincoln Home National Historic Site. The president's personal copy of the "Life of Black Hawk" was photographed inside the Cup (5).

[TOP & ABOVE] Coach Joel Quenneville joins (from left to right) former Bears defensive end Richard Dent, Bulls Chairman Jerry Reinsdorf and White Sox pitcher Mark Buerhle in a celebration of Chicago's sports champions at U.S. Cellular Field on Aug. 27, 2010.

[OPPOSITE TOP LEFT] The Cup sits next to Abraham Lincoln's personal desk at the Lincoln Home National Historic Site. Lincoln did much of his legal work and early political campaigning at this desk.

[OPPOSITE TOP RIGHT] The Stanley Cup on historic Route 66 near Bloomington, Ill. The legendary highway originally ran from Chicago through the Midwest and Southwest before ending in Los Angeles, Calif.

[OPPOSITE BOTTOM] At the Abraham Lincoln Book Shop in Chicago, the Cup rests on the Victorian table where the surrender documents ending the Civil War were prepared.

[TOP] Toby Keith serenades the Stanley Cup during a concert at First Midwest Bank Amphitheatre on Sept. 18, 2010.
[ABOVE] "Mr. Goalie" Glenn Hall joins the Stanley Cup on the balcony during the opening ceremony of the 2010 Blackhawks Convention.
[OPPOSITE TOP LEFT] Captain Jonathan Toews shows off the Stanley Cup to the Soldier Field crowd at the Bears 2010 season opener.
[OPPOSITE TOP RIGHT] The Stanley Cup joined the Notre Dame Band on the field before the Fighting Irish/Stanford Cardinal football game.
[OPPOSITE BOTTOM] From left to right, President John McDonough, Northwestern football coach Pat Fitzgerald, Executive Vice President Jay Blunk and Chairman Rocky Wirtz.

CHICAGO

CHICAGO BLACKHAWKS
2010 STANLEY CUP
CHAMPIONS

5

4

The Stanley Cup is just as iconic to hockey as some of Chicago's famed landmarks are to the Windy City. The silver chalice visited many of Chicago's most recognizable attractions, including the Chicago Theatre (1), Buckingham Fountain (2), John Hancock Observatory (3), the shore of Lake Michigan near Adler Planetarium (4) and the Art Institute (6), plus took a Wendella boat tour of the Chicago River (5). "We were standing unharnessed on top of the sixth-tallest building in the country," said Blackhawks photography coordinator Chase Agnello-Dean of the John Hancock Observatory shoot. "All that was separating the Stanley Cup and us from an 1,100 ft.-plummet was a little buffer zone of steel I-beam."

Oct. 9, 2010 — "Officially bringing the Cup back to the United Center was a pretty cool thing," said Blackhawks captain Jonathan Toews. So cool in fact that Toews described it as getting to experience, for a second, what it would have been like to win the Stanley Cup on home ice instead of in Philadelphia. Five members of the 1961 championship squad, including Stan Mikita and Bobby Hull — who wore #16 then — were on hand to pass the torch, delivering the 2010 Stanley Cup Champions banner to 13 members of the current roster who helped end Chicago's 49-year drought. "We brought in new management, new players, and made a commitment to you, our fans, that we would win the Stanley Cup. And guess what? We did," said Chairman Rocky Wirtz in an address to the capacity crowd. "It's amazing what happens when we all work together towards one goal. Just one goal."

THE HARDWARE

2010 STANLEY CUP CHAMPION CHICAGO BLACKHAWKS

Stanley Cup

CHICAGO BLACKHAWKS 2009 10

W. ROCKWELL WIRTZ JOHN MCDONOUGH JAY BLUNK
STAN BOWMAN AL MACISAAC KEVIN CHEVELDAYOFF SCOTTY BOWMAN
DALE TALLON JOEL QUENNEVILLE MIKE HAVILAND
JOHN TORCHETTI STEPHANE WAITE MIKE GAPSKI TROY PARCHMAN
JEFF THOMAS CLINT REIF PAWEL PRYLINSKI JIM HEINTZELMAN
PAUL GOODMAN PAUL VINCENT BRAD ALDRICH MARC BERGEVIN
MARK KELLEY NORM MACIVER MICHEL DUMAS RON ANDERSON
TONY OMMEN MARK BERNARD DR. MICHAEL TERRY

JONATHAN TOEWS CAPT. DAVE BOLLAND NICK BOYNTON
TROY BROUWER ADAM BURISH DUSTIN BYFUGLIEN
BRIAN CAMPBELL BEN FAGER COLIN FRASER JORDAN HENDRY
NIKLAS HJALMARSSON MARIAN HOSSA CRISTOBAL HUET
PATRICK KANE DUNCAN KEITH TOMAS KOPECKY ANDREW LADD
JOHN MADDEN ANTTI NIEMI BRENT SEABROOK PATRICK SHARP
BRENT SOPEL KRIS VERSTEEG

Stanley Cup Ring

STANLEY CUP

TOEWS

19

Conn Smythe Trophy

CONN-SMYTHE TROPHY

2008-2009
VGENI MALKIN
TTSBURGH PENGUINS

2009-2010
JONATHAN TOEWS
CHICAGO BLACKHAWKS

Norris Trophy

Campbell Bowl

Winter Olympics Medals

CHAPTER SIX
CONSISTENCY OF EXCELLENCE

CONSISTENCY OF EXCELLENCE BY BOB VERDI

When John McDonough was named president of the Blackhawks on Nov. 20, 2007, he knew his job would be challenging. But despite exercising due diligence, even he did not fully grasp the enormity of his task.

"It was like taking over an 80-year-old expansion team," McDonough recalled wistfully. One could argue that the situation was worse than that. At the very least, an expansion team can enjoy the warm embrace of a captive, hungry audience, anxious for games to be played in a vibrant new market, with a honeymoon period an integral part of the equation.

Alas, the Blackhawks were gasping for air, fighting apathy in a competitive sports landscape and atrophy on the ice. Indeed, after a 59-point season in 2003-04 — a franchise low since 1957-58 — the NHL shut down for 2004-05, yet it was as though hockey's fan base in Chicago, such as it was, did not miss scores and highlights a bit.

That residue of disenchantment is what McDonough inherited, along with a front office he perceived to be lacking in spirit, initiative and purpose. The cupboard was not totally bare because some talented players were in the system, but even they, by osmosis, felt as empty as the United Center about an organization that required a heart transplant on top of a complete attitude adjustment.

Only the most committed optimist could imagine that, by the spring of 2010, the Blackhawks would earn a Stanley Cup and see drastic increases in sponsorship and ticket revenue during McDonough's brief tenure, which coincided with the most serious economic freefall since the Depression. Come September, the Blackhawks had sold out of tickets for their opening Training Camp Festival, prompting coach Joel Quenneville to muse, "How do I run a practice in front of 20,000 fans?" It was a nice

"problem" to have, for sure, and one that seemed utterly unfathomable until McDonough altered the overall environment to such an extent that the modern hymn about how a "culture change" is imperative for upward mobility does not suffice.

McDonough, however, will be the first to admit that this mission implausible would not have materialized without the resources and vision of Chairman Rocky Wirtz. Owners of professional sports franchises tend not to mingle with the public — and for good reason. They tend not to be liked. That Rocky Wirtz invalidated that theorem about 15 minutes after taking control of the Blackhawks on Oct. 5, 2007, serves as just another example of how one man, with passion and a plan, can effect the resurrection of a woebegone hockey team and direct it to a championship inside three years.

When his father Bill, a Hall of Fame builder and team president for four decades, passed away, Rocky was overseeing the vast family business interests — wine and spirits distribution, insurance, real estate and banking. They were successful and profitable, and Rocky needed no introduction among movers and shakers, in Chicago or beyond. But, as per the line of succession, Rocky inherited one sector of the Wirtz heirloom that was struggling. The Blackhawks, once mighty and beloved, were drifting toward irrelevance. If they were a sleeping giant, as some observers in the National Hockey League believed, the Blackhawks had overdone their hibernation.

They were losing customers by the droves and bleeding money. With Bill hospitalized, Rocky received an emergency message: The Blackhawks were at the point of fiscal exhaustion and required an immediate transfusion of $34 million just to make payroll and put players on the ice for the 2007-08 season. Given that alarming information, Rocky could have been excused, upon his sudden and life-altering call to duty, for operating in a deliberate fashion and requesting patience. He might have said things that chairmen in distress say, things like "rebuilding" and "five-year plan" and "we are assessing our situation and will form a committee to discuss our options so as to become competitive again."

Rocky Wirtz did none of the above. "I knew we had to do something quickly," he said. "And we had to do something dramatic."

Was it ever. It didn't happen overnight. It only seemed that way. Well before the Stanley Cup celebration in the Loop on June 11, 2010, the machinations of Wirtz and McDonough had registered throughout the cutthroat industry of North American sports leagues. In 2004 ESPN ranked every franchise in baseball, football, basketball and hockey. The Blackhawks finished dead last. But in the spring of 2009, *Forbes Magazine* published a story, "The Greatest Sports-Business Turnaround Ever." It was about those same Blackhawks, albeit same in name only. The article described how "the changes have been breathtaking and comprehensive, quickly impacting every part of the team's business, perception and on-ice performance."

Little wonder why, at that Cup parade, hundreds of thousands of sunbaked bystanders hailed the chairman as the savior with chants of "ROCK-Y, ROCK-Y, ROCK-Y!" It is that way,

too, at the United Center, whenever his face is shown on the Jumbotron. You don't need a search party to find him either. Rocky could watch his hockey team in relative seclusion, ensconced in a suite above the red line, midst a security detail and finger sandwiches.

Instead Rocky sits among the people, in open air, open to suggestions, but mostly sincere thanks from the fans who have come back inside from the cold after too many losing winters. "It's almost embarrassing," says Rocky of the adulation he receives for "just doing my job."

Rocky implemented serial master strokes, none more crucial or timely than his impulse to schedule that initial meeting with McDonough, whose 24-year tenure in the executive branch with the Cubs was synonymous with elevating Wrigley Field to a destination point. They used to close the upper deck on weekends at the Friendly Confines for lack of interest. Under McDonough's reign, sellouts became routine.

McDonough thought he was being asked to lunch so Rocky might pick his brain. Somewhere between the soup and salad, McDonough realized there was more on the table. He agonized for a week or so — baseball, after all, was a significant slice of his adulthood. Finally, about six weeks into Rocky's reign, McDonough joined the Blackhawks as team president.

"I knew what I didn't know about hockey, same as I knew what I didn't know about baseball," said McDonough, who surveyed the Blackhawks executive branch and discovered a twig. There was no receptionist. Human resources director? What's that? In the old days, folks curious about purchasing season tickets were instructed to call the main switchboard and "ask for Mildred."

Instantly McDonough built from the ground up. Pat Foley, the popular broadcaster, was brought back and dozens of sales and marketing personnel brought in. Scouts were hired and sent on their way, around the globe in search of the next generation of Blackhawks.

From Day One, Wirtz and McDonough talked about a Stanley Cup, not making the playoffs. They talked about growing revenue, not trimming costs. They talked about restoring pride in the jersey, not about overpaying a veteran on his last legs to patch a roster hole. Kevin Cheveldayoff, assistant general manager and senior director of hockey operations, nailed it: Some franchises view player development as an expense; the new Blackhawks view it as an investment.

"We wanted to build an organization," McDonough said. "This is not just a hockey team. We were woefully short in many areas, from the way we treated our players, past and present, to how we traveled to our practice facilities. We needed to achieve a higher level of sophistication and professionalism. Players are your product, and you have to treat them with respect. You have to go above and beyond to put them in a situation to win. I couldn't believe that we didn't have a team physician on the road, for instance, perhaps to cut corners. We had to make it known that business would be done differently in Chicago. Fortunately I found that word travels fast around the NHL.

"Our hockey people and our business people operate as one. There is no division when it comes to what we want to achieve. That is how you build toward consistency of excellence. We speak one language. And if you ask me to give myself a grade, I would say 'incomplete' because our organization is still under construction."

The born-again Blackhawks endeared themselves to fans by televising a few home games during Rocky's first season at the helm. Then, in April of 2008, another dramatic announcement: Every game, home and away, 82 in all, would now be televised, including 20 on WGN Channel 9, the huge local independent that reaped boffo ratings for hockey back in the glory days. Bill Wirtz had stridently opposed showing home games on TV in Chicago.

"I'd say, 'Dad, we're losing generations of fans,'" recalled Rocky. "He said it wouldn't be fair to our fans with season tickets. But we'd gotten down to 3,400 or so just before he passed. And maybe half of them weren't going to the games. So we weren't televising home games for 1,700 people? Why bang your head against the wall?"

[OPPOSITE] From left to right: President John McDonough, Chairman Rocky Wirtz and Executive Vice President Jay Blunk.
Photo courtesy of David Durochik, *Sports Business Journal*.

DEFINING MOMENT

BLACKHAWKS AMBASSADORS: EMBRACING YOUR PAST by BOB VERDI

S hortly after being installed as president of the Blackhawks, John McDonough began gathering telephone numbers. During his front office reign with the Cubs, he was aware that several hockey players had left Chicago's Original Six franchise in a bad way. These awkward or acrimonious departures tainted the team's history and, by extension, affected fans who hurt for their bygone heroes and wondered why they were not part of the mix.

"One of our first objectives was to let it be known that we were out of the grudge business," recalled McDonough. "You can't have a meaningful present or a strong future if you are at war with your past."

Soon management announced that four Blackhawks Hall of Famers — Bobby Hull, Stan Mikita, Tony Esposito and later, Denis Savard — would serve as official "ambassadors," performing a variety of duties, including personal appearances and autograph sessions, but most of all, helping to heal a fracture between the team and fans.

"For one reason or another, we just didn't feel especially welcome in the building or around the

Blackhawks after we retired," said Mikita, who spent his entire career (1958-1980) with the club. "But that all changed."

McDonough's initial gesture was toward Hull, who logged 15 glorious seasons with the Blackhawks before he jumped to the Winnipeg Jets of the World Hockey Association in 1972. "The Golden Jet" had been brought back for a couple of cameos in the Chicago Stadium and United Center, but, like Mikita, was not a visible presence.

"Bobby and I were on the phone for about two hours, and most of the conversation was one-way, if you know what I mean," said McDonough. "I put my listening skills to good use." Hull also discussed his situation with Rocky Wirtz, the new team chairman, who confirmed McDonough's doctrine. After briefly mulling the offer, Hull accepted.

"Leaving the Blackhawks was the worst mistake I ever made, and I never thought I would be back," said Hull. "A lot of bridges were burned, and I had made some statements over time that weren't too kind to the Blackhawks. But I felt a tremendous void without them over a period of more than 30 years, and Rocky and John will never know what this has meant to my family and me. That phone call changed my life."

Hull and Mikita — who collected 604 and 541 goals respectively for the Blackhawks — were introduced as ambassadors at a United Center ceremony on March 7, 2008. A couple weeks later they were joined by Esposito, who played 15 seasons ('1969-1984) in goal for the Blackhawks, winning a franchise record 418 victories. But he retired with little fanfare and assumed front office roles with the Pittsburgh Penguins and Tampa Bay Lightning.

"It's great to be back with the Blackhawks," said Esposito. "They do everything first class, and even before they won the Stanley Cup, you could see how the new management had brought hockey to where it used to be in Chicago."

Savard, the fourth most prolific goal scorer (377) in Blackhawks annals, became the fourth ambassador in November of 2008.

"Rocky and John didn't owe me anything," said Savard. "Instead they have made me part of the family and treated me like gold. I only want to do this forever."

Since Wirtz and McDonough designated icons as ambassadors, other teams in Chicago have followed their lead. The Bulls named Scottie Pippen to a similar role; likewise the White Sox with Frank Thomas. Connecting with their legends had nothing to do with how the Blackhawks fared on the ice, but it had everything to do with altering the culture of the organization.

Of course, there was the possibility that Hull would politely decline. What then? "One thing I can assure you of about Bobby," said McDonough, "I wasn't going to take no for an answer."

[ABOVE] The Blackhawks' four ambassadors join the starters on the ice for the national anthem before the 2009-10 home opener.
[OPPOSITE] From left to right: Tony Esposito, Stan Mikita, Bobby Hull and Denis Savard suit up for a trial run of their opening night appearance.

That is as far as Rocky ever ventured in commenting on the old-school philosophy of his father. In fact, Rocky expressed admiration and respect for Bill. When interrogated about whether he was being disloyal by countermanding his father's policies, Rocky offered a perfectly airtight response: If Dad were still with us, I would hope that he feels I'm doing whatever is best to enhance the family business.

Bingo. And business boomed. Season subscribers currently top 14,000, and there is now an estimable waiting list. It's not a list of people waiting to be convinced that the Blackhawks are for real again. The waiting list is for tickets. Just like old times when the Stadium rocked and rolled from standing room only customers in the second balcony to the glass down below.

In January of 2008, McDonough hired a gifted sidekick from the Cubs, Jay Blunk, to run the business operation. His mission was to build the Blackhawk brand, and to say that Blunk has instituted a marketing machine is to vastly understate a body of work that is the envy of every professional sports franchise.

The Blackhawks in 2008-09 established an NHL record by drawing an average of 21,783 fans per home game, not counting the 40,818 who attended the New Year's Day Winter Classic at Wrigley Field, a mega-event. A new radio flagship station, all 50,000 watts of Chicago's WGN Radio 720, came aboard. Merchandise sales increased by more than 300 percent over a three-year span. TV ratings were so prodigious they could have passed for typographical errors. Dozens of sponsors were added, as was a Training Camp Festival and a Heritage Series honoring former Blackhawks on selected home dates. The Blackhawks were everywhere in traditional and new media. The team's website, with behind-the-scenes features from Blackhawks TV, buzzed 24/7, and promotional partnerships were forged with civic groups, plus the Cubs and White Sox.

When, or if, McDonough and Blunk take a vacation, or even sleep, is unclear. But the era of a summer sabbatical is past. Once upon a time, NHL teams turned out the lights for an entire month after the season. The Hawks never rest.

Some of their efforts are highly visible and seriously overdue. Four Hall of Fame ambassadors — Bobby Hull, Stan Mikita, Tony Esposito and Denis Savard — were brought back into the franchise fabric in 2008. But other gestures are performed behind the scenes. The Blackhawks possess a vibrant staff of employees, average age around 31, and if you doubt their intent on being fan-friendly, win or lose, ask a season ticketholder about that random phone call in the middle of January. "Is everything OK? Are you pleased?"

Last winter the Blackhawks Standbys were designated as the team's official fan club. Members soon were commissioned to pass out questionnaires about whether United Center spectators were satisfied with the experience, the food, the restrooms. With all due respect to previous regimes, pre-Rocky-McDonough-Blunk, some of us are ancient enough to remember when "the experience" of attending a Blackhawks game did not entail sharing our opinions.

Leaders do not conduct polls on inner sanctum issues, and the club's resurgence required difficult personnel choices to be made behind the Blackhawks bench and within hockey operations.

"Sometimes you need to make tough decisions that you strongly believe are in the best long-term interest of the franchise," McDonough explained.

Stan Bowman, a front office fixture since 2001, didn't require an adjustment period when McDonough installed him as the new general manager. His seat barely warm, Bowman embarked on signing three of the team's young stars — Jonathan Toews, Patrick Kane and Duncan Keith — to long-term deals. Bowman reminded fans that the league's hard salary cap would necessitate significant roster alterations at season's end, but he resisted the opportunity to ease payroll stress during the season — another tough decision. He could have traded, say, Dustin Byfuglien and Kris Versteeg in January, but would the Blackhawks have won the Cup without them?

Upon reviewing the first championship for the Blackhawks since 1961, Bowman aptly described the gamble as worthy, adding that the team had been somewhat of an anomaly. Toews, Kane and Keith had contributed mightily to the Cup by earning less than $4 million total, a statistical improbability that allowed the Blackhawks a surfeit of depth.

"Our youngest players were among our best," said Bowman, who at 36 became the youngest GM ever to win a Stanley Cup. "In 99 percent of the cases around the league, that isn't so. That enabled us to pay a third line center $3 million. But, starting with the 2010-11 season, the new scale for Toews, Kane and Keith make it different. There are no tricks to avoid a hard cap. Every team in the league deals with it."

But even in the NHL, there is a cap only on brawn, not brains. Witness the spectre of Stan's father, Scotty, another prime mover in a Blackhawks front office that is loaded. As senior advisor to hockey operations, Scotty participated in his twelfth Stanley Cup, a 35-pound jug that captain Toews raised on June 9, 2010, in the Wachovia Center. Toews kept his distance from the Clarence Campbell Bowl when the Blackhawks defeated San Jose to win the Western Conference, and he seemed somewhat disinterested in the Conn Smythe Trophy he earned as most valuable individual for the playoffs.

But Captain Serious was expressive when he latched onto that Stanley Cup because it represented the crowning achievement for a 22-year-old who established himself as the quiet leader in a locker room nourished by extraordinary chemistry. Toews never dabbled in the "I" formation. It was always "we." Character cannot be taught; it must be vested within. And the manner in which Toews carried and comported himself belied his age.

At the 2010 Blackhawks Convention, Toews resisted every opportunity for self-absorption. Instead he thanked fans in a jammed Chicago Hilton ballroom for their support. There is little mystery why Toews and the Blackhawks took over the city again, just like old times. They not only won the Stanley Cup, they shared it. □

[ABOVE] From left to right: Assistant General Manager/Senior Director, Hockey Operations Kevin Cheveldayoff; Executive Vice President Jay Blunk; Vice President/ General Manager Stan Bowman; Vice President/Assistant to the President Al MacIsaac; President John McDonough.

 **AFTERWORD** BY RICHARD M. DALEY

W

e've heard a lot about "the resurgent Chicago Blackhawks" over the past few years, about how hockey has finally found its way again in Chicago. But the truth is that Chicago has always been a hockey town and a Blackhawks town. It just may not always have known it.

Although Chicago is one of the largest, most sophisticated cities in the world, at its heart it's a small, working-class town; above all else, we value dedication, loyalty and heritage. We pride ourselves on a never-say-die attitude and embrace anyone who is willing to reach out to the community. Chicagoans are passionate about their sports teams and respect any athlete who gives 100 percent every game. We're a city of hard work, teamwork and never giving up; it's what Chicago — and the Blackhawks — stand for.

Even in the franchise's darkest days, Chicago was hungry for the Blackhawks to succeed. I heard the way fans reminisced about the glory days of Bobby Hull, Stan Mikita and Tony Esposito, and I shared those feelings. I remembered the roar of the old Chicago Stadium and the thrill of watching players such as Denis Savard and Jeremy Roenick. I watched eagerly as Jonathan Toews, Patrick Kane and a new generation of fresh faces debuted at the United Center. The seeds had been planted; Chicago just needed a reason to love the Blackhawks again.

But even I didn't realize how deeply the roots had taken hold until the 2010 Stanley Cup run. Throughout the playoffs I heard stories of Chicagoans who had never watched hockey before obsessing over the action and cheering each of the Hawks' 16 wins. Everywhere I turned I saw people wearing Blackhawks hats and t-shirts. Polyester hockey sweaters were suddenly fashionable even in Chicago's humid summer months. Just as the team so impressively represented the city at the highest levels of competition, the people of Chicago proudly supported their team in return.

Finally the Blackhawks' legions of fans were rewarded for their loyalty and passion. Rocky Wirtz and John McDonough have proven that with good leadership and a commitment to the fans, anything is possible. Since taking over they've made the Blackhawks a team that Chicago wants to root for and one they want to see succeed. From Duncan Keith and Brent Seabrook to Patrick Sharp and Marian Hossa, those guys play for themselves, their teammates and the city.

After the Blackhawks won the championship, I was one of the 2 million fans who gathered downtown for the parade. As far as I could see, the city was literally draped in red, and fans were crammed onto rooftops and looking out every window just to get a glimpse of hockey's ultimate prize.

The Blackhawks may have brought the Stanley Cup back home after 49 years, but at least for that day, it belonged to every Chicagoan.

— Richard M. Daley is the mayor of the city of Chicago